Memorabilia

XENOPHON

BOOK I

I

I have often wondered by what arguments those who indicted[1] Socrates could have persuaded the Athenians that his life was justly forfeit to the state. The indictment was to this effect: "Socrates is guilty of crime in refusing to recognise the gods acknowledged by the state, and importing strange divinities of his own; he is further guilty of corrupting the young."

[1] {oi grapsamenoi} = Meletus (below, IV. iv. 4, viii. 4; "Apol." 11, 19), Anytus ("Apol." 29), and Lycon. See Plat. "Apol." II. v. 18; Diog. Laert. II. v. (Socr.); M. Schanz, "Plat. Apol. mit deutschen Kemmentar, Einleitung," S. 5 foll.

In the first place, what evidence did they produce that Socrates refused to recognise the gods acknowledged by the state? Was it that he did not sacrifice? or that he dispensed with divination? On the contrary, he was often to be seen engaged in sacrifice, at home or at the common altars of the state. Nor was his dependence on divination less manifest. Indeed that saying of his, "A divinity[2] gives me a sign," was on everybody's lips. So much so that, if I am not mistaken, it lay at the root of the imputation that he imported novel divinities; though there was no greater novelty in his case than in that of other believers in oracular help, who commonly rely on omens of all sorts: the flight or cry of birds, the utterances of man, chance meetings,[3] or a victim's entrails. Even according to the popular conception, it is not the mere fowl, it is not the chance individual one meets, who knows what things are profitable for a man, but it is the gods who vouchsafe by such instruments to signify the same. This was also the tenet of Socrates. Only, whereas men ordinarily speak of being turned aside, or urged onwards by birds, or other creatures encountered on the path, Socrates suited his language to his conviction. "The divinity," said he, "gives me a sign." Further, he would constantly advise his associates to do this, or beware of doing that, upon the authority of this same divine voice; and, as a matter of fact, those who listened to his warnings prospered, whilst he who turned a deaf ear to them repented afterwards.[4] Yet, it will be readily conceded, he would hardly desire to present himself to his everyday companions in the character of either knave or fool. Whereas he would have appeared to be both, supposing[5] the God-given revelations had but revealed his own proneness to deception. It is plain he would not have ventured on forecast at all, but for his belief that the words he spoke would in fact be verified. Then on whom, or what, was the assurance rooted, if not upon God? And if he had faith in the gods, how could he fail to recognise them?

[2] Or, "A divine something." See "Encyc. Brit." "Socrates." Dr. H. Jackason; "The Daemon of Socrates," F. W. H. Myers; K. Joel, "Der echte und der Xenophontische Sokrates," i. p. 70 foll.; cf. Aristot. "M. M." 1182 a 10.
[3] See Aesch. "P. V." 487, {enodious te sombolous}, "and pathway tokens," L. Campbell; Arist. "Birds," 721, {sombolon ornin}: "Frogs," 196, {to sometukhon exion}; "Eccl." 792; Hor. "Od." iii. 27, 1-7.
[4] See "Anab." III. i. 4; "Symp." iv. 48.
[5] Or, "if his vaunted manifestations from heaven had but manifested the falsity of his judgment."

But his mode of dealing with his intimates has another aspect. As regards the ordinary necessities of life,[6] his advice was, "Act as you believe[7] these things may best be done." But in the case of those darker problems, the issues of which are incalculable, he directed his friends to consult the oracle, whether the business should be undertaken or not. "No one," he would say, "who wishes to manage a house or city with success: no one aspiring to guide the helm of state aright, can afford to dipense with aid from above. Doubtless, skill in carpentering, building, smithying, farming, of the art of governing men, together with the theory of these processes, and the sciences of arithmetic, economy, strategy, are affairs of study, and within the grasp of human intelligence. Yet there is a side even of these, and that not the least important, which the gods reserve to themselves, the bearing of which is hidden from mortal vision. Thus, let a man sow a field or plant a farm never so well, yet he cannot foretell who will gather in the fruits: another may build him a house of fairest proportion, yet he knows not who will inhabit it. Neither can a general foresee whether it will profit him to conduct a campaign, nor a politician be certain whether his leadership will turn to evil or good. Nor can the man who weds a fair wife, looking forward to joy, know whether through her he shall not reap sorrow. Neither can he who has built up a powerful connection in the state know whether he shall not by means of it be cast out of his city. To suppose that all these matters lay within the scope of human judgment, to the exclusion of the preternatural, was preternatural folly. Nor was it less extravagant to go and consult the will of Heaven on any questions which it is given to us to decide by dint of learning. As though a man should inquire, "Am I to choose an expert driver as my coachman, or one who has never handled the reins?" "Shall I appoint a mariner to be skipper of my vessel, or a landsman?" And so with respect to all we may know by numbering, weighing, and measuring. To seek advice from Heaven on such points was a sort of profanity. "Our duty is plain," he would observe; "where we are permitted to work through our natural faculties, there let us by all means apply them. But in things which are hidden, let us seek to gain knowledge from above, by divination; for the gods," he added, "grant signs to those to whom they will be gracious."

[6] Or, "in the sphere of the determined," {ta anagkaia} = certa, quorum eventus est necessarius; "things positive, the law-ordained department of life," as we might say. See Grote, "H. G." i. ch. xvi. 500 and passim.

[7] Reading {os nomizoien}, or if {os enomizen}, translate "As to things with certain results, he advised them to do them in the way in which he believed they would be done best"; i.e. he did not say, "follow your conscience," but, "this course seems best to me under the circumstances."

Again, Socrates ever lived in the public eye; at early morning he was to be seen betaking himself to one of the promenades, or wrestling- grounds; at noon he would appear with the gathering crowds in the market-place; and as day declined, wherever the largest throng might be encountered, there was he to be found, talking for the most part, while any one who chose might stop and listen. Yet no one ever heard him say, or saw him do anything impious or irreverent. Indeed, in contrast to others he set his face against all discussion of such high matters as the nature of the Universe; how the "kosmos," as the savants[8] phrase it, came into being;[9] or by what forces the celestial phenomena arise. To trouble one's brain about such matters was, he argued, to play the fool. He would ask first: Did these investigators feel their knowledge of things human so complete that they betook themselves to these lofty speculations? Or did they maintain that they were playing their proper parts in thus neglecting the affairs of man to speculate on the concerns of God? He was astonished they did not see how far these problems lay beyond mortal ken; since even those who pride themselves most on their discussion of these points differ from each other, as madmen do. For just as some madmen, he said, have no apprehension of what is truly terrible, others fear where no fear is; some are ready to say and do anything in public without the slightest symptom of shame;[10] others think they ought not so much as to set foot among their fellow-men; some honour neither temple, nor altar, nor aught else sacred to the name of God; others bow down to stocks and stones and worship the very beasts: - so is it with those thinkers whose minds are cumbered with cares[11] concerning the Universal Nature. One sect[12] has discovered that Being is one and indivisible. Another[13] that it is infinite in number. If one[14] proclaims that all things are in a continual flux, another[15] replies that nothing can possibly be moved at any time. The theory of the universe as a process of birth and death is met by the counter theory, that nothing ever could be born or ever will die.

[8] Lit. "the sophists." See H. Sidgwick, "J. of Philol." iv. 1872; v. 1874.

[9] Reading {ephu}. Cf. Lucian, "Icaromenip." xlvi. 4, in imitation of this passage apparently; or if {ekhei}, translate "is arranged." See Grote, "H. G." viii. 573.

[10] See "Anab." V. iv. 30.

[11] See Arist. "Clouds," 101, {merimnophrontistai kaloi te kagathoi}.

[12] e.g. Xenophanes and Parmenides, see Grote, "Plato," I. i. 16 foll.

[13] e.g. Leucippus and Democritus, ib. 63 foll.

[14] e.g. Heraclitus, ib. 27 foll.

[15] e.g. Zeno, ib. ii. 96.

But the questioning of Socrates on the merits of these speculators sometimes took another form. The student of human learning expects, he said, to make something of his studies for the benefit of himself or others, as he likes. Do these explorers into the divine operations hope that when they have discovered by what forces the various phenomena occur, they will create winds and waters at will and fruitful seasons? Will they manipulate these and the like to suit their needs? or has no such notion perhaps ever entered their heads, and will they be content simply to know how such things come into existence? But if this was his mode of describing those who meddle with such matters as these, he himself never wearied of discussing human topics. What is piety? what is impiety? What is the beautiful? what the ugly? What the noble? what the base? What are meant by just and unjust? what by sobriety and madness? what by courage and cowardice? What is a state? what is a statesman? what is a ruler over men? what is a ruling character? and other like problems, the knowledge of which, as he put it, conferred a patent of nobility on the possessor,[16] whereas those who lacked the knowledge might deservedly be stigmatised as slaves.

[16] Or, "was distinctive of the 'beautiful and good.'" For the phrase see below, ii. 2 et passim.

Now, in so far as the opinions of Socrates were unknown to the world at large, it is not surprising that the court should draw false conclusions respecting them; but that facts patent to all should have been ignored is indeed astonishing.

At one time Socrates was a member of the Council,[17] he had taken the senatorial oath, and sworn "as a member of that house to act in conformity with the laws." It was thus he chanced to be President of the Popular Assembly,[18] when that body was seized with a desire to put the nine[19] generals, Thrasyllus, Erasinides, and the rest, to death by a single inclusive vote. Whereupon, in spite of the bitter resentment of the people, and the menaces of several influential citizens, he refused to put the question, esteeming it of greater importance faithfully to abide by the oath which he had taken, than to gratify the people wrongfully, or to screen himself from the menaces of the mighty. The fact being, that with regard to the care bestowed by the gods upon men, his belief differed widely from that of the multitude. Whereas most people seem to imagine that the gods know in part, and are ignorant in part, Socrates believed firmly that the gods know all things - both the things that are said and the things that are done, and the things that are counselled in the silent chambers of the heart. Moreover, they are present everywhere, and bestow signs upon man concerning all the things of man.

[17] Or "Senate." Lit. "the Boule."

[18] Lit. "Epistates of the Ecclesia." See Grote, "H. G." viii. 271; Plat. "Apol." 32 B.

[19] {ennea} would seem to be a slip of the pen for {okto}, eight. See "Hell." I. v. 16; vi. 16; vi. 29; vii. 1 foll.

I can, therefore, but repeat my former words. It is a marvel to me how the Athenians came to be persuaded that Socrates fell short of sober- mindedness as touching the gods. A man who never ventured one impious word or deed against the gods we worship, but whose whole language concerning them, and his every act, closely coincided, word for word, and deed for deed, with all we deem distinctive of devoutest piety.

II

No less surprising to my mind is the belief that Socrates corrupted the young. This man, who, beyond what has been already stated, kept his appetites and passions under strict control, who was pre-eminently capable of enduring winter's cold and summer's heat and every kind of toil, who was so schooled to curtail his needs that with the scantiest of means he never lacked sufficiency - is it credible that such a man could have made others irreverent or lawless, or licentious, or effeminate in face of toil? Was he not rather the saving of many through the passion for virtue which he roused in them, and the hope he infused that through careful management of themselves they might grow to be truly beautiful and good - not indeed that he ever undertook to be a teacher of virtue, but being evidently virtuous himself he made those who associated with him hope that by imitating they might at last resemble him.

But let it not be inferred that he was negligent of his own body or approved of those who neglected theirs. If excess of eating, counteracted by excess of toil, was a dietary of which he disapproved,[1] to gratify the natural claim of appetite in conjunction with moderate exercise was a system he favoured, as tending to a healthy condition of the body without trammelling the cultivation of the spirit. On the other hand, there was nothing dandified or pretentious about him; he indulged in no foppery of shawl or shoes, or other effeminacy of living.

[1] See [Plat.] "Erast." 132 C.

Least of all did he tend to make his companions greedy of money. He would not, while restraining passion generally, make capital out of the one passion which attached others to himself; and by this abstinence, he believed, he was best consulting his own freedom; in so much that he stigmatised those who condescended to take wages for their society as vendors of their own persons, because they were compelled to discuss for the benefits of their paymasters. What surprised him was that any one possessing virtue should deign to ask money as its price instead of simply finding his rward in the acquisition of an honest friend, as if the new-fledged soul of honour could forget her debt of gratitude to her greatest benefactor.

For himself, without making any such profession, he was content to believe that those who accepted his views would play their parts as good and true friends to himself and one another their lives long. Once more then: how should a man of this character corrupt the young? unless the careful cultivation of virtue be corruption.

But, says the accuser,[2] by all that's sacred! did not Socrates cause his associates to despise the established laws when he dwelt on the folly of appointing state officers by ballot?[3] a principle which, he said, no one would care to apply in selecting a pilot or a flute- player or in any similar case, where a mistake would be far less disastrous than in matters political. Words like these, according to the accuser, tended to incite the young to contemn the established constitution, rendering them violent and headstrong. But for myself I think that those who cultivate wisdom and believe themselves able to instruct their fellow-citizens as to their interests are least likely to become partisans of violence. They are too well aware that to violence attach enmities and dangers, whereas results as good may be obtained by persuasion safely and amicably. For the victim of violence hates with vindictiveness as one from whom something precious has been stolen, while the willing subject of persuasion is ready to kiss the hand which has done him a service. Hence compulsion is not the method of him who makes wisdom his study, but of him who wields power untempered by reflection. Once more: the man who ventures on violence needs the support of many to fight his battles, while he whose strength lies in persuasiveness triumphs single-handed, for he is conscious of a cunning to compel consent unaided. And what has such a one to do with the spilling of blood? since how ridiculous it were to do men to death rather than turn to account the trusty service of the living.

[2] {o kategoros} = Polycrates possibly. See M. Schantz, op. cit., "Einleitun," S. 6: "Die Anklagerede des Polykrates"; Introduction, p. xxxii. foll.
[3] i.e. staking the election of a magistrate on the colour of a bean. See Aristot. "Ath. Pol." viii. 2, and Dr. Sandys ad loc.

But, the accuser answers, the two men[4] who wrought the greatest evils to the state at any time - to wit, Critias and Alcibiades - were both companions of Socrates - Critias the oligarch, and Alcibiades the democrat. Where would you find a more arrant thief, savage, and murderer[5] than the one? where such a portent of insolence, incontinence, and high-handedness as the other? For my part, in so far as these two wrought evil to the state, I have no desire to appear as the apologist of either. I confine myself to explaining what this intimacy of theirs with Socrates really was.

[4] See "Hell." I. and II. passim.
[5] Reading {kleptistatos te kai biaiotatos kai phonikotatos}, or if {pleonektistatos te kai biaiotatis}, translate "such a manner of greed and violence as the one, of insolence, etc., as the other?" See Grote, "H. G." viii. 337.

Never were two more ambitious citizens seen at Athens. Ambition was in their blood. If they were to have their will, all power was to be in their hands; their fame was to eclipse all other. Of Socrates they knew - first that he lived an absolutely independent life on the scantiest means; next that he was self-disciplined to the last degree in respect of pleasures; lastly that he was so formidable in debate that there was no antagonist he could not twist round his little finger. Such being their views, and such the character of the pair, which is the more probable: that they sought the society of Socrates because they felt the fascination of his life, and were attracted by the bearing of the man? or because they thought, if only we are leagued with him we shall become adepts in statecraft and unrivalled in the arts of speech and action? For my part I believe that if the choice from Heaven had been given them to live such a life as they saw Socrates living to its close, or to die, they would both have chosen death.

Their acts are a conclusive witness to their characters. They no sooner felt themselves to be the masters of those they came in contact with than they sprang aside from Socrates and plunged into that whirl of politics but for which they might never have sought his society.

It may be objected: before giving his companions lessons in politics Socrates had better have taught them sobriety.[6] Without disputing the principle, I would point out that a teacher cannot fail to discover to his pupils his method of carrying out his own precepts, and this along with argumentative encouragement. Now I know that Socrates disclosed himself to his companions as a beautiful and noble being, who would reason and debate with them concerning virtue and other human interests in the noblest manner. And of these two I know that as long as they were companions of Socrates even they were temperate, not assuredly from fear of being fined or beaten by Socrates, but because they were persuaded for the nonce of the excellence of such conduct.

[6] {sophrosune} = "sound-mindedness," "temperence." See below, IV. Iii. 1.

Perhaps some self-styled philosophers[7] may here answer: "Nay, the man truly just can never become unjust, the temperate man can never become intemperate, the man who has learnt any subject of knowledge can never be as though he had learnt it not." That, however, is not my own conclusion. It is with the workings of the soul as with those of the body; want of exercise of the organ leads to inability of function, here bodily, there spiritual, so that we can neither do the things that we should nor abstain from the things we should not. And that is why fathers keep their sons, however temperate they may be, out of the reach of wicked men, considering that if the society of the good is a training in virtue so also is the society of the bad its dissolution.

[7] In reference to some such tenet as that of Antisthenes ap. Diog. Laert. VI. ix. 30, {areskei d' autois kai ten areten didakten einai, katha phesin 'Antisthenes en to 'Rraklei kai anapobleton uparkhein}. Cf. Plat. "Protag." 340 D, 344 D.

To this the poet[8] is a witness, who says:
"From the noble thou shalt be instructed in nobleness; but, and if thou minglest with the base thou wilt destroy what wisdom thou hast now";
And he[9] who says:
"But the good man has his hour of baseness as well as his hour of virtue" -
to whose testimony I would add my own. For I see that it is impossible to remember a long poem without practice and repetition; so is forgetfulness of the words of instruction engendered in the heart that has ceased to value them. With the words of warning fades the recollection of the very condition of mind in which the soul yearned after holiness; and once forgetting this, what wonder that the man should let slip also the memory of virtue itself! Again I see that a man who falls into habits of drunkenness or plunges headlong into licentious love, loses his old power of practising the right and abstaining from the wrong. Many a man who has found frugality easy whilst passion was cold, no sooner falls in love than he loses the faculty at once, and in his prodigal expenditure of riches he will no longer withhold his hand from gains which in former days were too base to invite his touch. Where then is the difficulty of supposing that a man may be temperate to-day, and to-morrow the reverse; or that he who once has had it in his power to act virtuously may not quite lose that power?[10] To myself, at all events, it seems that all beautiful and noble things are the result of constant practice and training; and pre-eminently the virtue of temperance, seeing that in one and the same bodily frame pleasures are planted and spring up side by side with the soul and keep whispering in her ear, "Have done with self- restraint, make haste to gratify us and the body."[11]

[8] Theognis, 35, 36. See "Symp." ii. 4; Plat. "Men." 95 D.
[9] The author is unknown. See Plat. "Protag." l.c.
[10] Cf. "Cyrop." V. i. 9 foll.; VI. i. 41.
[11] See my remarks, "Hellenica Essays," p. 371 foll.

But to return to Critias and Alcibiades, I repeat that as long as they lived with Socrates they were able by his support to dominate their ignoble appetites;[12] but being separated from him, Critias had to fly to Thessaly,[13] where he consorted with fellows better versed in lawlessness than justice. And Alcibiades fared no better. His personal beauty on the one hand incited bevies of fine ladies[14] to hunt him down as fair spoil, while on the other hand his influence in the state and among the allies exposed him to the corruption of many an adept in the arts of flattery; honoured by the democracy and stepping easily to the front rank he behaved like an athlete who in the games of the Palaestra is so assured of victory that he neglects his training; thus he presently forgot the duty which he owed himself.

[12] Cf. [Plat.] "Theag." 130 A.
[13] See "Hell." II. iii. 36.
[14] Cf. Plut. "Ages.," "Alcib."

Such were the misadventures of these two. Is the sequel extraordinary? Inflated with the pride of ancestry,[15] exalted by their wealth, puffed up by power, sapped to the soul's core by a host of human tempters, separate moreover for many a long day from Socrates - what wonder that they reached the full stature of arrogancy! And for the offences of these two Socrates is to be held responsible! The accuser will have it so. But for the fact that in early days, when they were both young and of an age when dereliction from good feeling and self- restraint might have been expected, this same Socrates kept them modest and well-behaved, not one word of praise is uttered by the accuser for all this. That is not the measure of justice elsewhere meted. Would a master of the harp or flute, would a teacher of any sort who has turned out proficient pupils, be held to account because one of them goes away to another teacher and turns out to be a failure? Or what father, if he have a son who in the society of a certain friend remains an honest lad, but falling into the company of some other becomes a good-for-nothing, will that father straightway accuse the earlier instructor? Will not he rather, in proportion as the boy deteriorates in the company of the latter, bestow more heartfelt praise upon the former? What father, himself sharing the society of his own children, is held to blame for their transgressions, if only his own goodness be established? Here would have been a fair test to apply to Socrates: Was he guilty of any base conduct himself? If so let him be set down as a knave, but if, on the contrary, he never faltered in sobriety from beginning to end, how in the name of justice is he to be held to account for a baseness which was not in him?

[15] Or, "became overweening in arrogance." Cf. "Henry VIII. II. iv. 110": "But your heart is crammed with arrogancy, spleen, and pride."

I go further: if, short of being guilty of any wrong himself, he saw the evil doings of others with approval, reason were he should be held blameworthy. Listen then: Socrates was well aware that Critias was attached to Euthydemus,[16] aware too that he was endeavouring to deal by him after the manner of those wantons whose love is carnal of the body. From this endeavour he tried to deter him, pointing out how illiberal a thing it was, how ill befitting a man of honour to appear as a beggar before him whom he loved, in whose eyes he would fain be precious, ever petitioning for something base to give and base to get.

[16] See below, IV. ii. 1 (if the same person).

But when this reasoning fell on deaf ears and Critias refused to be turned aside, Socrates, as the story goes, took occasion of the presence of a whole company and of Euthydemus to remark that Critias appeared to be suffering from a swinish affection, or else why this desire to rub himself against Euthydemus like a herd of piglings scraping against stones.

The hatred of Critias to Socrates doubtless dates from this incident. He treasured it up against him, and afterwards, when he was one of the Thirty and associated with Charicles as their official lawgiver, [17] he framed the law against teaching the art of words[18] merely from a desire to vilify Socrates. He was at a loss to know how else to lay hold of him except by levelling against him the vulgar charge[19] against philosophers, by which he hoped to prejudice him with the public. It was a charge quite unfounded as regards Socrates, if I may judge from anything I ever heard fall from his lips myself or have learnt about him from others. But the animus of Critias was clear. At the time when the Thirty were putting citizens, highly respectable citizens, to death wholesale, and when they were egging on one man after another to the commission of crime, Socrates let fall an observation: "It would be sufficiently extraordinary if the keeper of a herd of cattle[20] who was continually thinning and impoverishing his cattle did not admit himself to be a sorry sort of herdsman, but that a ruler of the state who was continually thinning and impoverishing the citizens should neither be ashamed nor admit himself to be a sorry sort of ruler was more extraordinary still." The remark being reported to the government, Socrates was summoned by Critias and Charicles, who proceeded to point out the law and forbade him to converse with the young. "Was it open to him," Socrates inquired of the speaker, "in case he failed to understand their commands in any point, to ask for an explanation?"

[17] Lit. "Nomothetes." See "Hell." II. iii. 2; Dem. 706. For Charicles see Lys. "c. Eratosth." S. 56; Aristot. "Pol." v. 6. 6.

[18] See Diog. Laert. II. v. ("Socr.")

[19] i.e. {to ton etto logon kreitto poiein}, "of making the worse appear the better cause." Cf. Arist. "Clouds."

[20] See Dio Chrys. "Or." 43.

"Certainly," the two assented.

Then Socrates: I am prepared to obey the laws, but to avoid transgression of the law through ignorance I need instruction: is it on the supposition that the art of words tends to correctness of statement or to incorrectness that you bid us abstain from it? for if the former, it is clear we must abstain from speaking correctly, but if the latter, our endeavour should be to amend our speech.

To which Charicles, in a fit of temper, retorted: In consideration of your ignorance,[21] Socrates, we will frame the prohibition in language better suited to your intelligence: we forbid you to hold any conversation whatsoever with the young.

[21] See Aristot. "de Soph. El." 183 b7.

Then Socrates: To avoid all ambiguity then, or the possibility of my doing anything else than what you are pleased to command, may I ask you to define up to what age a human being is to be considered young?

For just so long a time (Charicles answered) as he is debarred from sitting as a member of the Council,[22] as not having attained to the maturity of wisdom; accordingly you will not hold converse with any one under the age of thirty.

[22] The Boule or Senate. See W. L. Newman, "Pol. Aristot." i. 326.

Soc. In making a purchase even, I am not to ask, what is the price of this? if the vendor is under the age of thirty?

Cha. Tut, things of that sort: but you know, Socrates, that you have a way of asking questions, when all the while you know how the matter stands. Let us have no questions of that sort.

Soc. Nor answers either, I suppose, if the inquiry concerns what I know, as, for instance, where does Charicles live? or where is Critias to be found?

Oh yes, of course, things of that kind (replied Charicles), while Critias added: But at the same time you had better have done with your shoemakers, carpenters, and coppersmiths.[23] These must be pretty well trodden out at heel by this time, considering the circulation you have given them.

[23] Cf. Plat. "Gorg." 491 A; "Symp." 221 E; Dio Chrys. "Or." 55, 560 D, 564 A.

Soc. And am I to hold away from their attendant topics also - the just, the holy, and the like?

Most assuredly (answered Charicles), and from cowherds in particular; or else see that you do not lessen the number of the herd yourself.

Thus the secret was out. The remark of Socrates about the cattle had come to their ears, and they could not forgive the author of it.

Perhaps enough has been said to explain the kind of intimacy which had subsisted between Critias and Socrates, and their relation to one another. But I will venture to maintain that where the teacher is not pleasing to the pupil there is no education. Now it cannot be said of Critias and Alcibiades that they associated with Socrates because they found him pleasing to them. And this is true of the whole period. From the first their eyes were fixed on the headship of the state as their final goal. During the time of their imtimacy with Socrates there were no disputants whom they were more eager to encounter than professed politicians.

Thus the story is told of Alcibiades - how before the age of twenty he engaged his own guardian, Pericles, at that time prime minister of the state, in a discussion concerning laws.

Alc. Please, Pericles, can you teach me what a law is?

Per. To be sure I can.

Alc. I should be so much obliged if you would do so. One so often hears the epithet "law-abiding" applied in a complimentary sense; yet, it strikes me, one hardly deserves the compliment, if one does not know what a law is.

Per. Fortunately there is a ready answer to your difficulty. You wish to know what a law is? Well, those are laws which the majority, being met together in conclave, approve and enact as to what it is right to do, and what it is right to abstain from doing.

Alc. Enact on the hypothesis that it is right to do what is good? or to do what is bad?

Per. What is good, to be sure, young sir, not what is bad.

Alc. Supposing it is not the majority, but, as in the case of an oligarchy, the minority, who meet and enact the rules of conduct, what are these?

Per. Whatever the ruling power of the state after deliberation enacts as our duty to do, goes by the name of laws.

Alc. Then if a tyrant, holding the chief power in the state, enacts rules of conduct for the citizens, are these enactments law?

Per. Yes, anything which a tyrant as head of the state enacts, also goes by the name of law.

Alc. But, Pericles, violence and lawlessness - how do we define them? Is it not when a stronger man forces a weaker to do what seems right to him - not by persuasion but by compulsion?

Per. I should say so.

Alc. It would seem to follow that if a tyrant, without persuading the citizens, drives them by enactment to do certain things - that is lawlessness?

Per. You are right; and I retract the statement that measures passed by a tyrant without persuasion of the citizens are law.

Alc. And what of measures passed by a minority, not by persuasion of the majority, but in the exercise of its power only? Are we, or are we not, to apply the term violence to these?

Per. I think that anything which any one forces another to do without persuasion, whether by enactment or not, is violence rather than law.

Alc. It would seem that everything which the majority, in the exercise of its power over the possessors of wealth, and without persuading them, chooses to enact, is of the nature of violence rather than of law?

To be sure (answered Pericles), adding: At your age we were clever hands at such quibbles ourselves. It was just such subtleties which we used to practise our wits upon; as you do now, if I mistake not.

To which Alcibiades replied: Ah, Pericles, I do wish we could have met in those days when you were at your cleverest in such matters.

Well, then, as soon as the desired superiority over the politicians of the day seemed to be attained, Critias and Alcibiades turned their backs on Socrates. They found his society unattractive, not to speak of the annoyance of being cross-questioned on their own shortcomings. Forthwith they devoted themselves to those affairs of state but for which they would never have come near him at all.

No; if one would seek to see true companions of Socrates, one must look to Crito,[24] and Chaerephon, and Chaerecrates, to Hermogenes, to Simmias and Cebes, to Phaedondes and others, who clung to him not to excel in the rhetoric of the Assembly or the law-courts, but with the nobler ambition of attaining to such beauty and goodliness of soul as would enable them to discharge the various duties of life to house and family, to relatives and friends, to fellow-citizens, and to the state at large. Of these true followers not one in youth or old age was ever guilty, or thought guilty, of committing any evil deed.

[24] For these true followers, familiar to us in the pages of Plato, ("Crito," "Apol.," "Phaedo," etc) see Cobet, "Pros. Xen."

"But for all that," the accuser insists, "Socrates taught sons to pour contumely upon their fathers[25] by persuading his young friends that he could make them wiser than their sires, or by pointing out that the law allowed a son to sue his father for aberration of mind, and to imprison him, which legal ordinance he put in evidence to prove that it might be well for the wiser to imprison the more ignorant."

[25] See "Apol." 20; Arist. "Clouds," 1407, where Pheidippides "drags his father Strepsiades through the mire."

Now what Socrates held was, that if a man may with justice incarcerate another for no better cause than a form of folly or ignorance, this same person could not justly complain if he in his turn were kept in bonds by his superiors in knowledge; and to come to the bottom of such questions, to discover the difference between madness and ignorance was a problem which he was perpetually working at. His opinion came to this: If a madman may, as a matter of expediency to himself and his friends, be kept in prison, surely, as a matter of justice, the man who knows not what he ought to know should be content to sit at the feet of those who know, and be taught.

But it was the rest of their kith and kin, not fathers only (according to the accuser), whom Socrates dishonoured in the eyes of his circle of followers, when he said that "the sick man or the litigant does not derive assistance from his relatives,[26] but from his doctor in the one case, and his legal adviser in the other." "Listen further to his language about friends," says the accuser: "'What is the good of their being kindly disposed, unless they can be of some practical use to you? Mere goodness of disposition is nothing; those only are worthy of honour who combine with the knowledge of what is right the faculty of expounding it;'[27] and so by bringing the young to look upon himself as a superlatively wise person gifted with an extraordinary capacity for making others wise also, he so worked on the dispositions of those who consorted with him that in their esteem the rest of the world counted for nothing by comparison with Socrates."

[26] See Grote, "H. G." v. 535.
[27] Cf. Thuc. ii. 60. Pericles says, "Yet I with whom you are so angry venture to say of myself, that I am as capable as any one of devising and explaining a sound policy." - Jowett.

Now I admit the language about fathers and the rest of a man's relations. I can go further, and add some other sayings of his, that "when the soul (which is alone the indwelling centre of intelligence) is gone out of a man, be he our nearest and dearest friend, we carry the body forth and bury it out of sight." "Even in life," he used to say, "each of us is ready to part with any portion of his best possession - to wit, his own body - if it be useless and unprofitable. He will remove it himself, or suffer another to do so in his stead. Thus men cut off their own nails, hair, or corns; they allow surgeons to cut and cauterise them, not without pains and aches, and are so grateful to the doctor for his services that they further give him a fee. Or again, a man ejects the spittle from his mouth as far as possible.[28] Why? Because it is of no use while it stays within the system, but is detrimental rather."

MEMORABILIA

[28] See Aristot. "Eth. Eud." vii. 1.

Now by these instances his object was not to inculcate the duty of burying one's father alive or of cutting oneself to bits, but to show that lack of intelligence means lack of worth;[29] and so he called upon his hearers to be as sensible and useful as they could be, so that, be it father or brother or any one else whose esteem he would deserve, a man should not hug himself in careless self-interest, trusting to mere relationship, but strive to be useful to those whose esteem he coveted.

[29] i.e. "witless and worthless are synonymous."

But (pursues the accuser) by carefully culling the most immoral passages of the famous poets, and using them as evidences, he taught his associates to be evildoers and tyrranical: the line of Hesiod[30] for instance -
No work is a disgrace; slackness of work is the disgrace -
"interpreted," says the accuser, "by Socrates as if the poet enjoined us to abstain from no work wicked or ignoble; do everything for the sake of gain."

[30] "Works and Days," 309 {'Ergon d' ouden oneidos}. Cf. Plat. "Charm." 163 C.

Now while Socrates would have entirely admitted the propositions that "it is a blessing and a benefit to a man to be a worker," and that "a lazy do-nothing is a pestilent evil," that "work is good and idleness a curse," the question arises, whom did he mean by workers? In his vocabulary only those were good workmen[31] who were engaged on good work; dicers and gamblers and others engaged on any other base and ruinous business he stigmatised as the "idle drones"; and from this point of view the quotation from Hesiod is unimpeachable -
No work is a disgrace; only idlesse is disgrace.
But there was a passage from Homer[32] for ever on his lips, as the accuser tells us - the passage which says concerning Odysseus,
What prince, or man of name, He found flight-giv'n, he would restrain with words of gentlest blame: "Good sir, it fits you not to fly, or fare as one afraid, You should not only stay yourself, but see the people stayed."
Thus he the best sort us'd; the worst, whose spirits brake out in noise,[33] He cudgell'd with his sceptre, chid, and said, "Stay, wretch, be still, And hear thy betters; thou art base, and both in power and skill Poor and unworthy, without name in counsel or in war." We must not all be kings.

[31] See below, III. ix. 9.
[32] "Il." ii. 188 foll., 199 foll. (so Chapman).
[33] Lit. "But whatever man of the people he saw and found him shouting." - W. Leaf.

The accuser informs us that Socrates interpreted these lines as though the poet approved the giving of blows to commoners and poor folk. Now no such remark was ever made by Socrates; which indeed would have been tantamount to maintaining that he ought to be beaten himself. What he did say was, that those who were useful neither in word nor deed, who were incapable of rendering assistance in time of need to the army or the state or the people itself, be they never so wealthy, ought to be restrained, and especially if to incapacity they added effrontery.
As to Socrates, he was the very opposite of all this - he was plainly a lover of the people, and indeed of all mankind. Though he had many ardent admirers among citizens and strangers alike, he never demanded any fee for his society from any one,[34] but bestowed abundantly upon all alike of the riches of his sould - good things, indeed, of which fragments accepted gratis at his hands were taken and sold

at high prices to the rest of the community by some,[35] who were not, as he was, lovers of the people, since with those who had not money to give in return they refused to discourse. But of Socrates be it said that in the eyes of the whole world he reflected more honour on the state and a richer lustre than ever Lichas,[36] whose fame is proverbial, shed on Lacedaemon. Lichas feasted and entertained the foreign residents in Lacedaemon at the Gymnopaediae most handsomely. Socrates gave a lifetime to the outpouring of his substance in the shape of the greatest benefits bestowed on all who cared to receive them. In other words, he made those who lived in his society better men, and sent them on their way rejoicing.

[34] See "Symp." iv. 43; Plat. "Hipp. maj." 300 D; "Apol." 19 E.
[35] See Diog. Laert. II. viii. 1.
[36] See "Hell." III. ii. 21; Thuc. v. 50; Plut. "Cim." 284 C. For the Gymnopaediae, see Paus. III. xi. 9; Athen. xiv. p. 631.

To no other conclusion, therefore, can I come but that, being so good a man, Socrates was worthier to have received honour from the state than death. And this I take to be the strictly legal view of the case, for what does the law require?[37] "If a man be proved to be a thief, a filcher of clothes, a cut-purse, a housebreaker, a man-stealer, a robber of temples, the penalty is death." Even so; and of all men Socrates stood most aloof from such crimes.

[37] See "Symp." iv. 36; Plat. "Rep." 575 B; "Gorg." 508 E.

To the state he was never the cause of any evil - neither disaster in war, nor faction, nor treason, nor any other mischief whatsoever. And if his public life was free from all offence, so was his private. He never hurt a single soul either by deprivation of good or infliction of evil, nor did he ever lie under the imputation of any of those misdoings. WHere then is his liability to the indictment to be found? Who, so far from disbelieving in the gods, as set forth in the indictment, was conspicuous beyond all men for service to heaven; so far from corrupting the young - a charge alleged with insistence by the prosecutor - was notorious for the zeal with which he strove not only to stay his associates from evil desires, but to foster in them a passionate desire for that loveliest and queenliest of virtues without which states and families crumble to decay.[38] Such being his conduct, was he not worthy of high honour from the state of Athens?

[38] Or, "the noblest and proudest virtue by means of which states and families are prosperously directed."

III

It may serve to illustrate the assertion that he benefited his associates partly by the display of his own virtue and partly by verbal discourse and argument, if I set down my various recollections[1] on these heads. And first with regard to religion and the concerns of heaven. In conduct and language his behaviour conformed to the rule laid down by the Pythia[2] in reply to the question, "How shall we act?" as touching a sacrifice or the worship of ancestors, or any similar point. Her answer is: "Act according to the law and custom of your state, and you will act piously." After this pattern Socrates behaved himself, and so he exhorted others to behave, holding them to be but busybodies and vain fellows who acted on any different principle.

[1] Hence the title of the work, {'Apomenmoneumata}, "Recollections, Memoirs, Memorabilia." See Diog. Laert. "Xen." II. vi. 48.

[2] The Pythia at Delphi.

His formula or prayer was simple: "Give me that which is best for me," for, said he, the gods know best what good things are - to pray for gold or silver or despotic power were no better than to make some particular throw at dice or stake in battle or any such thing the subject of prayer, of which the future consequences are manifestly uncertain.[3]

[3] See (Plat.) "Alcib. II." 142 foll.; Valerius Max. vii. 2; "Spectator," No. 207.

If with scant means he offered but small sacrifices he believed that he was in no wise inferior to those who make frequent and large sacrifices from an ampler store. It were ill surely for the very gods themselves, could they take delight in large sacrifices rather than in small, else oftentimes must the offerings of bad men be found acceptable rather than of good; nor from the point of view of men themselves would life be worth living if the offerings of a villain rather than of a righteous man found favour in the sight of Heaven. His belief was that the joy of the gods is greater in proportion to the holiness of the giver, and he was ever an admirer of that line of Hesiod which says,
According to thine ability do sacrifice to the immortal gods.[4]

[4] Hesiod, "Works and Days," 336. See "Anab." III. ii. 9.

"Yes," he would say, "in our dealings with friends and strangers alike, and in reference to the demands of life in general, there is no better motto for a man than that: 'let a man do according to his ability.'"
Or to take another point. If it appeared to him that a sign from heaven had been given him, nothing would have induced him to go against heavenly warning: he would as soon have been persuaded to accept the guidance of a blind man ignorant of the path to lead him on a journey in place of one who knew the road and could see; and so he denounced the folly of others who do things contrary to the warnings of God in order to avoid some disrepute among men. For himself he despised all human aids by comparison with counsel from above.
The habit and style of living to which he subjected his soul and body was one which under ordinary circumstances[5] would enable any one adopting it to look existence cheerily in the face and to pass his days serenely: it would certainly entail no difficulties as regards expense. So frugal was it that a man must work little indeed who could not earn the quantum which contented Socrates. Of food he took just enough to make eating a pleasure - the appetite he brought to it was sauce sufficient; while as to drinks, seeing that he only drank when thirsty, any draught refreshed.[6] If he accepted an invitation to dinner, he had no difficulty in avoiding the common snare of over- indulgence, and his advice to people who could not equally control their appetite was to avoid taking what would allure them to eat if not hungry or to drink if not thirsty.[7] Such things are ruinous to the constitution, he said, bad for stomachs, brains, and soul alike; or as he used to put it, with a touch of sarcasm,[8] "It must have been by feasting men on so many dainty dishes that Circe produced her pigs; only Odysseus through his continency and the 'promptings[9] of Hermes' abstained from touching them immoderately, and by the same token did not turn into a swine." So much for this topic, which he touched thus lightly and yet seriously.

[5] {ei me ti daimonion eie}, "save under some divinely-ordained calamity." Cf. "Cyrop." I. vi. 18; "Symp." viii. 43.
[6] See "Ages." ix; Cic. "Tusc." v. 34, 97; "de Fin." ii. 28, 90.
[7] Cf. Plut. "Mor." 128 D; Clement, "Paedag." 2. 173, 33; "Strom." 2, 492, 24; Aelian, "N. A." 8, 9.
[8] "Half in gibe and half in jest," in ref. to "Od." x. 233 foll.: "So she let them in . . ."
[9] {upothemosune}, "inspiration." Cf. "Il." xv. 412; "Od." xvi. 233.

But as to the concerns of Aphrodite, his advice was to hold strongly aloof from the fascination of fair forms: once lay finger on these and it is not easy to keep a sound head and a sober mind. To take a particular case. It was a mere kiss which, as he had heard, Critobulus[10] had some time given to a fair youth, the son of Alcibiades.[11] Accordingly Critobulus being present, Socrates propounded the question.

[10] For Critobulus (the son of Crito) see "Econ." i. 1 foll.; "Symp." i. 3 foll.
[11] See Isocr. "Or." xvi. Cobet conj. {ton tou 'Axiokhou uion}, i.e. Clinias.

Soc. Tell me, Xenophon, have you not always believed Critobulus to be a man of sound sense, not wild and self-willed? Should you not have said that he was remarkable for his prudence rather than thoughtless or foolhardy?

Xen. Certainly that is what I should have said of him.

Soc. Then you are now to regard him as quite the reverse - a hot- blooded, reckless libertine: this is the sort of man to throw somersaults into knives,[12] or to leap into the jaws of fire.

[12] Cf. "Symp." ii. 10, iv. 16. See Schneider ad loc.

Xen. And what have you seen him doing, that you give him so bad a character?

Soc. Doing? Why, has not the fellow dared to steal a kiss from the son of Alcibiades, most fair of youths and in the golden prime?

Xen. Nay, then, if that is the foolhardy adventure, it is a danger which I could well encounter myself.

Soc. Pour soul! and what do you expect your fate to be after that kiss? Let me tell you. On the instant you will lose your freedom, the indenture of your bondage will be signed; it will be yours on compulsion to spend large sums on hurtful pleasures; you will have scarcely a moment's leisure left for any noble study; you will be driven to concern yourself most zealously with things which no man, not even a madman, would choose to make an object of concern.

Xen. O Heracles! how fell a power to reside in a kiss!

Soc. Does it surprise you? Do you not know that the tarantula, which is no bigger than a threepenny bit,[13] has only to touch the mouth and it will afflict its victim with pains and drive him out of his senses.

[13] Lit. "a half-obol piece." For the {phalaggion} see Aristot. "H. A." ix. 39, 1.

Xen. Yes, but then the creature injects something with its bite.

Soc. Ah, fool! and do you imagine that these lovely creatures infuse nothing with their kiss, simply because you do not see the poison? Do you not know that this wild beast which men call beauty in its bloom is all the more terrible than the tarantula in that the insect must first touch its victim, but this at a mere glance of thebeholder, without even contact, will inject something into him - yards away - which will make him man. And may be that is why the Loves are called "archers," because these beauties wound so far off.[14] But my advice to you, Xenophon, is, whenever you catch sight of one of these fair forms, to run helter-skelter for bare life without a glance behind; and to you, Critobulus, I would say, "Go abroad for a year: so long time will it take to heal you of this wound."

[14] L. Dindorf, etc. regard the sentence as a gloss. Cf. "Symp." iv. 26 [{isos de kai . . . entimoteron estin}].

Such (he said), in the affairs of Aphrodite, as in meats and drinks, should be the circumspection of all whose footing is insecure. At least they should confine themselves to such diet as the soul would dispense with, save for some necessity of the body; and which even so ought to set up no disturbance. [15] But for himself, it was clear, he was prepared at all points and invulnerable. He found less difficulty in abstaining from beauty's fairest and fullest bloom than many others from weeds and garbage. To sum up:[16] with regard to eating and drinking and these other temptations of the sense, the equipment of his soul made him independent; he could boast honestly that in his moderate fashion[17] his pleasures were no less than theirs who take such trouble to procure them, and his pains far fewer.

[15] Cf. "Symp." iv. 38.
[16] L. Dindorf [brackets] this passage as spurious.
[17] On the principle "enough is as good as a feast," {arkountos}.

IV

A belief is current, in accordance with views maintained concerning Socrates in speech and writing, and in either case conjecturally, that, however powerful he may have been in stimulating men to virtue as a theorist, he was incapable of acting as their guide himself.[1] It would be well for those who adopt this view to weigh carefully not only what Socrates effected "by way of castigation" in cross-questioning whose who conceived themselves to be possessed of all knowledge, but also his everyday conversation with those who spent their time in close intercourse with himself. Having done this, let them decide whether he was incapable of making his companions better.

[1] Al. "If any one believes that Socrates, as represented in certain dialogues (e.g. of Plato, Antisthenes, etc.) of an imaginary character, was an adept ({protrepsasthai}) in the art of stimulating people to virtue negatively but scarcely the man to guide ({proagein}) his hearers on the true path himself." Cf. (Plat.) "Clitophon," 410 B; Cic. "de Or." I. xlvii. 204; Plut. "Mor." 798 B. See Grote, "Plato," iii. 21; K. Joel, op. cit. p. 51 foll.; Cf. below, IV. Iii. 2.

I will first state what I once heard fall from his lips in a discussion with Aristodemus,[2] "the little," as he was called, on the topic of divinity.[3] Socrates had observed that Aristodemus neither sacrificed nor gave heed to divination, but on the contrary was disposed to ridicule those who did.

[2] See Plat. "Symp." 173 B: "He was a little fellow who never wore any shoes, Aristodemus, of the deme of Cydathenaeum." - Jowett.
[3] Or, "the divine element."

So tell me, Aristodemus (he begain), are there any human beings who have won your admiration for their wisdom?
Ar. There are.
Soc. Would you mention to us their names?
Ar. In the writings of epic poetry I have the greatest admiration for Homer. . . . And as a dithyrambic poet for Melanippides.[4] I admire also Sophocles as a tragedian, Polycleitus as a sculptor, and Zeuxis as a painter.

[4] Melanippides, 430 B.C. See Cobet, "Pros. Xen." s.n.

Soc. Which would you consider the more worthy of admiration, a fashioner of senseless images devoid of motion or one who could fashion living creatures endowed with understanding and activity?
Ar. Decidedly the latter, provided his living creatures owed their birth to design and were not the offspring of some chance.

Soc. But now if you had two sorts of things, the one of which presents no clue as to what it is for, and the other is obviously for some useful purpose - which would you judge to be the result of chance, which of design?

Ar. Clearly that which is produced for some useful end is the work of design.

Soc. Does it not strike you then that he who made man from the beginning[5] did for some useful end furnish him with his several senses - giving him eyes to behold the visible word, and ears to catch the intonations of sound? Or again, what good would there be in odours if nostrils had not been bestowed upon us? what perception of sweet things and pungent, and of all the pleasures of the palate, had not a tongue been fashioned in us as an interpreter of the same? And besides all this, do you not think this looks like a matter of foresight, this closing of the delicate orbs of sight with eyelids as with folding doors, which, when there is need to use them for any purpose, can be thrown wide open and firmly closed again in sleep? and, that even the winds of heaven may not visit them too roughly, this planting of the eyelashes as a protecting screen?[6] this coping of the region above the eyes with cornice-work of eyebrow so that no drop of sweat fall from the head and injure them? again this readiness of the ear to catch all sounds and yet not to be surcharged? this capacity of the front teeth of all animals to cut and of the "grinders" to receive the food and reduce it to pulp? the position of the mouth again, close to the eyes and nostrils as a portal of ingress for all the creature's supplies? and lastly, seeing that matter passing out[7] of the body is unpleasant, this hindward direction of the passages, and their removal to a distance from the avenues of sense? I ask you, when you see all these things constructed with such show of foresight can you doubt whether they are products of chance or intelligence?

[5] Cf. Aristot. "de Part. Animal." 1. For the "teleological" views see IV. iii. 2 foll.
[6] "Like a sieve" or "colander."
[7] "That which goeth out of a man."

Ar. To be sure not! Viewed in this light they would seem to be the handiwork of some wise artificer, [8] full of love for all things living.[9]

[8] "Demiurge."
[9] Passage referred to by Epictetus ap. Stob. "Flor." 121, 29.

Soc. What shall we say of this passion implanted in man to beget offspring, this passion in the mother to rear her babe, and in the creature itself, once born, this deep desire of life and fear of death?

Ar. No doubt these do look like the contrivances of some one deliberately planning the existence of living creatures.

Soc. Well, and doubtless you feel to have a spark of wisdom yourself?

Ar. Put your questions, and I will answer.

Soc. And yet you imagine that elsewhere no spark of wisdom is to be found? And that, too, when you know that you have in your body a tiny fragment only of the mighty earth, a little drop of the great waters, and of the other elements, vast in their extent, you got, I presume, a particle of each towards the compacting of your bodily frame? Mind alone, it would seem, which is nowhere to be found,[10] you had the lucky chance to snatch up and make off with, you cannot tell how. And these things around and about us, enormous in size, infinite in number, owe their orderly arrangement, as you suppose, to some vacuity of wit?

[10] Cf. Plat. "Phileb." 30 B: "Soc. May our body be said to have a soul? Pro. Clearly. Soc. And whence comes that soul, my dear Protarchus, unless the body of the universe, which contains elements similar to our bodies but finer, has also a soul? Can there be any other source?" - Jowett. Cic. "de N. D." ii. 6; iii. 11.

Ar. It may be, for my eyes fail to see the master agents of these, as one sees the fabricators of things produced on earth.

Soc. No more do you see your own soul, which is the master agent of your body; so that, as far as that goes, you may maintain, if you like, that you do nothing with intelligence,[11] but everything by chance.

[11] Or, "by your wit," {gnome}

At this point Aristodemus: I assure you, Socrates, that I do not disdain the Divine power. On the contrary, my belief is that the Divinity is too grand to need any service which I could render.

Soc. But the grander that power is, which deigns to tend and wait upon you, the more you are called upon to honour it.

Ar. Be well assured, if I could believe the gods take thought for all men, I would not neglect them.

Soc. How can you suppose that they do not so take thought? Who, in the first place, gave to man alone of living creatures his erect posture, enabling him to see farther in front of him and to contemplate more freely the height above, and to be less subject to distress than other creatures [endowed like himself with eyes and ears and mouth].[12] Consider next how they gave to the beast of the field[13] feet as a means of progression only, but to man they gave in addition hands - those hands which have achieved so much to raise us in the scale of happiness above all animals. Did they not make the tongue also? which belongs indeed alike to man and beast, but in man they fashioned it so as to play on different parts of the mouth at different times, whereby we can produce articulate speech, and have a code of signals to express our every want to one another. Or consider the pleasures of the sexual appetite; limited in the rest of the animal kingdom to certain seasons, but in the case of man a series prolonged unbroken to old age. Nor did it content the Godhead merely to watch over the interests of man's body. What is of far higher import, he implanted in man the noblest and most excellent type of soul. For what other creature, to begin with, has a soul to appreciate the existence of the gods who have arranged this grand and beauteous universe? What other tribe of animals save man can render service to the gods? How apt is the spirit of man to take precautions against hunger and thirst, cold and heat, to alleviate disease and foster strength! how suited to labour with a view to learning! how capable of garnering in the storehouse of his memory all that he has heard or seen or understood! Is it not most evident to you that by the side of other animals men live and move a race of gods - by nature excellent, in beauty of body and of soul supreme? For, mark you, had a creature of man's wit been encased in the body of an ox,[14] he would have been powerless to carry out his wishes, just as the possession of hands divorced from human wit is profitless. And then you come, you who have obtained these two most precious attributes, and give it as your opinion, that the gods take no thought or care for you. Why, what will you have them to do, that you may believe and be persuaded that you too are in their thoughts?

[12] See Kuhner for an attempt to cure the text.
[13] {erpetois}, a "poetical" word. Cf. "Od." iv. 418; Herod. i. 140.
[14] See Aristot. "de Part. Animal." iv. 10.

Ar. When they treat me as you tell us they treat you, and send me counsellors to warn me what I am to do and what abstain from doing,[15] I will believe.

[15] See IV. Iii. 12.

Soc. Send you counsellors! Come now, what when the people of Athens make inquiry by oracle, and the gods' answer comes? Are you not an Athenian? Think you not that to you also the answer is given? What when they send portents to forewarn the states of Hellas? or to all mankind? Are you not a man? a

Hellene? Are not these intended for you also? Can it be that you alone are excepted as a signal instance of Divine neglect? Again, do you suppose that the gods could have implanted in the heart of man the belief in their capacity to work him weal or woe had they not the power? Would not men have discovered the imposture in all this lapse of time? Do you not perceive that the wisest and most perdurable of human institutions - be they cities or tribes of men - are ever the most God-fearing; and in the individual man the riper his age and judgment, the deeper his religousness? Ay, my good sir (he broke forth), lay to heart and understand that even as your own mind within you can turn and dispose of your body as it lists, so ought we to think that the wisdom which abides within the universal frame does so dispose of all things as it finds agreeable to itself; for hardly may it be that your eye is able to range over many a league, but that the eye of God is powerless to embrace all things at a glance; or that to your soul it is given to dwell in thought on matters here or far away in Egypt or in Sicily, but that the wisdom and thought of God is not sufficient to include all things at one instant under His care. If only you would copy your own behaviour[16] where human beings are concerned. It is by acts of service and of kindness that you discover which of your fellows are willing to requite you in kind. It is by taking another into your counsel that you arrive at the secret of his wisdom. If, on like principle, you will but make trial of the gods by acts of service, whether they will choose to give you counsel in matters obscure to mortal vision, you shall discover the nature and the greatness of Godhead to be such that they are able at once to see all things and to hear all things and to be present everywhere, nor does the least thing escape their watchful care.

[16] Or, "reason as you are wont to do."

To my mind the effect of words like these was to cause those about him to hold aloof from unholiness, baseness, and injustice, not only whilst they were seen of men, but even in the solitary place, since they must believe that no part of their conduct could escape the eye of Heaven.

V

I suppose it may be taken as admitted that self-control is a noble acquirement for a man.[1] If so, let us turn and consider whether by language like the following he was likely to lead his listeners onwards[2] to the attainment of this virtue. "Sirs," he would say, "if a war came upon us and we wished to choose a man who would best help us to save ourselves and to subdue our enemy, I suppose we should scarcely select one whom we knew to be a slave to his belly, to wine, or lust, and prone to succumb to toil or sleep. Could we expect such an one to save us or to master our foes? Or if one of us were nearing the end of his days, and he wished to discover some one to whom he might entrust his sons for education, his maiden daughters for protection, and his property in general for preservation, would he deem a libertine worthy of such offices? Why, no one would dream of entrusting his flocks and herds, his storehouses and barns, or the superintendence of his works to the tender mercies of an intemperate slave. If a butler or an errand boy with such a character were offered to us we would not take him as a free gift. And if he would not accept an intemperate slave, what pains should the master himself take to avoid that imputation.[3] For with the incontinent man it is not as with the self-seeker and the covetous. These may at any rate be held to enrich themselves in depriving others. But the intemperate man cannot claim in like fashion to be a blessing to himself if a curse to his neighbours; nay, the mischief which he may cause to others is nothing by comparison with that which redounds against himself, since it is the height of mischief to ruin - I do not say one's own house and property - but one's own body and one's own soul. Or to take an example from social intercourse, no one cares for a guest who evidently takes more pleasure in the wine and the viands than in the friends beside him - who stints his comrades of the affection due to them to dote upon a mistress. Does it not come to this, that every honest man is bound to look upon self-restraint as the very corner-stone of virtue:[4] which he should seek to lay down as the basis and foundation of his soul? Without self-restraint who can lay any good lesson to heart or practise it when learnt in any degree worth speaking of? Or, to put it conversely, what slave of pleasure will not suffer degeneracy of soul and body? By Hera,[5] well may every free man pray to be saved from the service of such a slave; and well too may he who is in bondage to such pleasures supplicate Heaven to send him good masters, seeing that is the one hope of salvation left him."

[1] Lit. "a beautiful and brave possesion."
[2] {proubibaze}.
[3] Or, "how should the master himself beware lest he fall into that category."
[4] {krepida}. See Pind. "Pyth." iv. 138; ib. vii. 3; ib. fr. 93.
[5] See below, III. x. 9, xi. 5; IV. ii. 9, iv. 8; "Econ." x. 1; "Cyrop." I. iv. 12; Plat. "Phaedr." 230 B. Cf. Shakesp. "by'r Lakin."

Well-tempered words: yet his self-restraint shone forth even more in his acts than in his language. Not only was he master over the pleasures which flow from the body, but of those also which are fed by riches, his belief being that he who receives money from this or that chance donor sets up over himself a master, and binds himself to an abominable slavery.

VI

In this context some discussions with Antiphon the sophist[1] deserve record. Antiphon approaches Socrates in hope of drawing away his associates, and in their presence thus accosts him.

[1] {o teratoskopos}, "jealous of Socrates," according to Aristotle ap. Diog. Laert. II. v. 25. See Cobet, "Pros. Xen."

Antiphon. Why, Socrates, I always thought it was expected of students of philosophy to grow in happiness daily; but you seem to have reaped other fruits from your philosophy. At any rate, you exist, I do not say live, in a style such as no slave serving under a master would put up with. Your meat and your drink are of the cheapest sort, and as to clothes, you cling to one wretched cloak which serves you for summer and winter alike; and so you go the whole year round, without shoes to your feet or a shirt to your back. Then again, you are not for taking or making money, the mere seeking of which is a pleasure, even as the possession of it adds to the sweetness and independence of existence. I do not know whether you follow the common rule of teachers, who try to fashion their pupils in imitation of themselves,[2] and propose to mould the characters of your companions; but if you do you ought to dub yourself professor of the art of wretchedness.[3]

[2] Or, "try to turn out their pupils as copies of themselves."
[3] See Arist. "Clouds," {on o kakodaimon Sokrates kai Khairephon}.

Thus challenged, Socrates replied: One thing to me is certain, Antiphon; you have conceived so vivid an idea of my life of misery that for yourself you would choose death sooner than live as I do. Suppose now we turn and consider what it is you find so hard in my life. Is it that he who takes payment must as a matter of contract finish the work for which he is paid, whereas I, who do not take it, lie under no constraint to discourse except with whom I choose? Do you despise my dietary on the ground that the food which I eat is less wholesome and less stengthening than yours, or that the articles of my consumption are so scarce and so much costlier to procure than yours? Or have the fruits of your marketing a flavour denied to mine? Do you not know the sharper the appetite the less the need of sauces, the keener the thirst the less the desire for out-of-the-way drinks? And as to raiment, clothes, you know, are changed on account of cold or else of heat. People only wear boots and shoes in order not to gall their feet and be prevented walking. Now I ask you, have you ever noticed that I keep more within doors than others on account of the cold? Have you ever seen me battling with any one for shade on account of the heat? Do you not know that even a weakling by nature may, by dint of exercise and practice, come to outdo a giant who neglects his body? He will beat him in the particular point of training, and bear the strain more easily. But you apparently will not have it that I, who am for ever training myself to endure this, that, and the other thing which may befall the body, can brave all hardships more easily than yourself for instance, who perhaps are not so practised. And to escape slavery to the belly or to sleep or lechery, can you suggest more effective means than the possession of some powerful attraction, some counter-charm which shall gladden not only in the using, but by the hope enkindled of its lasting usefulness? And yet this you do know; joy is not to him who feels that he is doing well in nothing - it belongs to one who is persuaded that things are progressing with him, be it tillage or the working of a vessel,[4] or any of the thousand and one things on which a man may chance to be employed. To him it is given to rejoice as he reflects, "I am doing well." But is the pleasured derived from all these put together half as joyous as the consciousness of becoming better oneself, of acquiring better and better friends? That, for my part, is the belief I continue to cherish.

[4] "The business of a shipowner or skipper."

Again, if it be a question of helping one's friends or country, which of the two will have the larger leisure to devote to these objects - he who leads the life which I lead to-day, or he who lives in the style which you deem so fortunate? Which of the two will adopt a soldier's life more easily - the man who cannot get on without expensive living, or he to whom whatever comes to hand suffices? Which will be the readier to capitulate and cry "mercy" in a siege - the man of elaborate wants, or he who can get along happily with the readiest things to hand? You, Antiphon, would seem to suggest that happiness consists of luxury and extravagance; I hold a different creed. To have no wants at all is, to my mind, an attribute of Godhead;[5] to have as few wants as possible the nearest approach to Godhead; and as that which is divine is mightiest, so that is next mightiest which comes closest to the divine.

[5] Cf. Aristot. "Eth. N." x. viii. 1.

Returning to the charge at another time, this same Antiphon engaged Socrates in conversation thus.

Ant. Socrates, for my part, I believe you to be a good and upright man; but for your wisdom I cannot say much. I fancy you would hardly dispute the verdict yourself, since, as I remark, you do not ask a money payment for your society; and yet if it were your cloak now, or your house, or any other of your possessions, you would set some value upon it, and never dream, I will not say of parting with it gratis, but of exchanging it for less than its worth. A plain proof, to my mind, that if you thought your society worth anything, you would ask for it not less than its equivalent in gold.[6] Hence the conclusion to which I have come, as already stated: good and upright you may be, since you do not cheat people from pure selfishness; but wise you cannot be, since your knowledge is not worth a cent.

[6] Or rather "money," lit. "silver."

To this onslaught Socrates: Antiphon, it is a tenet which we cling to that beauty and wisdom have this in common, that there is a fair way and a foul way in which to dispose of them. The vendor of beauty purchases an evil name, but supposing the same person have discerned a soul of beauty in his lover and makes that man his friend, we regard his choice as sensible.[7] So is it with wisdom; he who sells it for money to the first bidder we name a sophist,[8] as though one should say a man who prostitutes his wisdom; but if the same man, discerning the noble nature of another, shall teach that other every good thing, and make him his friend, of such a one we say he does that which it is the duty of every good citizen of gentle soul to do. In accordance with this theory, I too, Antiphon, having my tastes, even as another finds pleasure in his horse and his hounds,[9] and another in his fighting cocks, so I too take my pleasure in good friends; and if I have any good thing myself I teach it them, or I commend them to others by whom I think they will be helped forwards on the path of virtue. The treasures also of the wise of old, written and bequeathed in their books,[10] I unfold and peruse in common with my friends. If our eye light upon any good thing we cull it eagerly, and regard it as great gain if we may but grow in friendship with one another.

[7] Add "and a sign of modesty," {sophrona nomizomen}.
[8] {sophistas}. See Grote, "H. G." viii. 482 foll.; "Hunting," xi. foll.
[9] Cf. Plat. "Lys." 211 E.
[10] Cf. "Symp." iv. 27.

As I listened to this talk I could not but reflect that he, the master, was a person to be envied, and that we, his hearers, were being led by him to beauty and nobility of soul.

Again on some occasion the same Antiphon asked Socrates how he expected to make politicians of others when, even if he had the knowledge, he did not engage in politics himself.

Socrates replied: I will put to you a question, Antiphon: Which were the more statesmanlike proceeding, to practise politics myself single- handed, or to devote myself to making as many others as possible fit to engage in that pursuit?

VII

Let us here turn and consider whether by deterring his associates from quackery and false seeming he did not directly stimulate them to the pursuit of virtue.[1] He used often to say there was no better road to renown than the one by which a man became good at that wherein he desired to be reputed good.[2] The truth of the concept he enforced as follows: "Let us reflect on what a man would be driven to do who wanted to be thought a good flute player, without really being so. He would be forced to imitate the good flute player in the externals of his art, would he not? and first or all, seeing that these artists always have a splendid equipment,[3] and travel about with a long train of attendants, he must have the same; in the next place, they can command the plaudits of a multitude, he therefore must pack a conclave of clackers. But one thing is clear: nothing must induce him to give a performance, or he will be exposed at once, and find himself a laughing-stock not only as a sorry sort of flute player, but as a wretched imposter. And now he has a host of expenses to meet; and not one advantage to be reaped; and worse than all his evil reputation. What is left him but to lead a life stale and unprofitable, the scorn and mockery of men? Let us try another case. Suppose a man wished to be thought a good general or a good pilot, though he were really nothing of the sort, let us picture to our minds how it will fare with him. Of two misfortunes one: either with a strong desire to be thought proficient in these matters, he will fail to get others to agree with him, which will be bad enough; or he will succeed, with worse result; since it stands to reason that anyone appointed to work a vessel or lead an army without the requisite knowledge will speedily ruin a number of people whom he least desires to hurt, and will make but a sorry exit from the stage himself." Thus first by one instance and then another would he demonstrate the unprofitableness of trying to appear rich, or courageous, or strong, without really being the thing pretended. "You are sure sooner or later to have commands laid upon you beyond your power to execute, and failing just where you are credited with capacity, the world will give you no commiseration." "I call that man a cheat, and a great cheat too," he would say, "who gets money or goods out of some one by persuasion, and defrauds him; but of all imposters he surely is the biggest who can delude people into thinking that he is fit to lead the state, when all the while he is a worthless creature."[4]

[1] {apotrepon proutrepen}. See K. Joel, op. cit. p. 450 foll.

[2] Cf. "Cyrop." I. vi. 22.

[3] Or, "furniture of the finest," like Arion's in Herod. i. 24. Schneid. cf. Demosth. 565. 6.

[4] Here follows the sentence [{emoi men oun edokei kai tou alazoneuesthai apotrepein tous sunontas toiade dialegomenos}], which, for the sake of convenience, I have attached to the first sentence of Bk. II. ch. i. [{edokei de moi . . . ponou.}] I believe that the commentators are right in bracketing both one and the other as editorial interpolations.

BOOK II

I

Now, if the effect of such discourses was, as I imagine, to deter his hearers from the paths of quackery and false-seeming,[1] so I am sure that language like the following was calculated to stimulate his followers to practise self-control and endurance: self-control in the matters of eating, drinking, sleeping, and the cravings of lust; endurance of cold and heat and toil and pain. He had noticed the undue licence which one of his acquaintances allowed himself in all such matters.[2] Accordingly he thus addressed him:

[1] This sentence in the Greek concludes Bk. I. There is something wrong or very awkward in the text here.
[2] Cf. Grote, "Plato," III. xxxviii. p. 530.

Tell me, Aristippus (Socrates said), supposing you had two children entrusted to you to educate, one of them must be brought up with an aptitude for government, and the other without the faintest propensity to rule - how would you educate them? What do you say? Shall we begin our inquiry from the beginning, as it were, with the bare elements of food and nutriment?

Ar. Yes, food to begin with, by all means, being a first principle,[3] without which there is no man living but would perish.

[3] Aristippus plays upon the word {arkhe}.

Soc. Well, then, we may expect, may we not, that a desire to grasp food at certain seasons will exhibit itself in both the children?

Ar. It is to be expected.

Soc. Which, then, of the two must be trained, of his own free will,[4] to prosecute a pressing business rather than gratify the belly?

[4] {proairesis}.

Ar. No doubt the one who is being trained to govern, if we would not have affairs of state neglected during[5] his government.

[5] Lit. "along of."

Soc. And the same pupil must be furnished with a power of holding out against thirst also when the craving to quench it comes upon him?

Ar. Certainly he must.

Soc. And on which of the two shall we confer such self-control in regard to sleep as shall enable him to rest late and rise early, or keep vigil, if the need arise?

Ar. To the same one of the two must be given that endurance also.

Soc. Well, and a continence in regard to matters sexual so great that nothing of the sort shall prevent him from doing his duty? Which of them claims that?

Ar. The same one of the pair again.

Soc. Well, and on which of the two shall be bestowed, as a further gift, the voluntary resolution to face toils rather than turn and flee from them?

Ar. This, too, belongs of right to him who is being trained for government.

Soc. Well, and to which of them will it better accord to be taught all knowledge necessary towards the mastery of antagonists?

Ar. To our future ruler certainly, for without these parts of learning all his other capacities will be merely waste.

Soc. [6]Will not a man so educated be less liable to be entrapped by rival powers, and so escape a common fate of living creatures, some of which (as we all know) are hooked through their own greediness, and often even in spite of a native shyness; but through appetite for food they are drawn towards the bait, and are caught; while others are similarly ensnared by drink?

[6] [SS. 4, 5, L. Dind. ed Lips.]

Ar. Undoubtedly.

Soc. And others again are victims of amorous heat, as quails, for instance, or partridges, which, at the cry of the hen-bird, with lust and expectation of such joys grow wild, and lose their power of computing dangers: on they rush, and fall into the snare of the hunter?

Aristippus assented.

Soc. And would it not seem to be a base thing for a man to be affected like the silliest bird or beast? as when the adulterer invades the innermost sanctum[7] of the house, though he is well aware of the risks which his crime involves,[8] the formidable penalties of the law, the danger of being caught in the toils, and then suffering the direst contumely. Considering all the hideous penalties which hang over the adulterer's head, considering also the many means at hand to release him from the thraldom of his passion, that a man should so drive headlong on to the quicksands of perdition[9] - what are we to say of such frenzy? The wretch who can so behave must surely be tormented by an evil spirit?[10]

[7] {eis as eirktas}. The penetralia.
[8] Or, "he knows the risks he runs of suffering those penalties with which the law threatens his crime should he fall into the snare, and being caught, be mutilated."
[9] Or, "leap headlong into the jaws of danger."
[10] {kakodaimonontos}.

Ar. So it strikes me.

Soc. And does it not strike you as a sign of strange indifference that, whereas the greater number of the indispensable affairs of men, as for instance, those of war and agriculture, and more than half the rest, need to be conducted under the broad canopy of heaven,[11] yet the majority of men are quite untrained to wrestle with cold and heat?

[11] Or, "in the open air."

Aristippus again assented.

Soc. And do you not agree that he who is destined to rule must train himself to bear these things lightly?

Ar. Most certainly.

Soc. And whilst we rank those who are self-disciplined in all these matters among persons fit to rule, we are bound to place those incapable of such conduct in the category of persons without any pretension whatsoever to be rulers?

Ar. I assent.

Soc. Well, then, since you know the rank peculiar to either section of mankind, did it ever strike you to consider to which of the two you are best entitled to belong?

Yes I have (replied Aristippus). I do not dream for a moment of ranking myself in the class of those who wish to rule. In fact, considering how serious a business it is to cater for one's own private needs, I look upon it as the mark of a fool not to be content with that, but to further saddle oneself with the duty of providing the rest of the community with whatever they may be pleased to want. That, at the cost of much personal enjoyment, a man should put himself at the head of a state, and then, if he fail to carry through every jot and tittle of that state's desire, be held to criminal account, does seem to me the very extravagance of folly. Why, bless me! states claim to treat their rulers precisely as I treat my domestic slaves. I expect my attendants to furnish me with an abundance of necessaries, but not to lay a finger on one of them themselves. So these states regard it as the duty of a ruler to provide them with all the good things imaginable, but to keep his own hands off them all the while.[12] So then, for my part, if anybody desires to have a heap of pother himself,[13] and be a nuisance to the rest of the world, I will educate him in the manner suggested, and he shall take his place among those who are fit to rule; but for myself, I beg to be enrolled amongst those who wish to spend their days as easily and pleasantly as possible.

[12] Or, "but he must have no finger in the pie himself."
[13] See Kuhner ad loc.

Soc. Shall we then at this point turn and inquire which of the two are likely to lead the pleasanter life, the rulers or the ruled?

Ar. By all means let us do so.

Soc. To begin then with the nations and races known to ourselves.[14] In Asia the Persians are the rulers, while the Syrians, Phrygians, Lydians are ruled; and in Europe we find the Scythians ruling, and the Maeotians being ruled. In Africa[15] the Carthaginians are rulers, the Libyans ruled. Which of these two sets respectively leads the happier life, in your opinion? Or, to come nearer home - you are yourself a Hellene - which among Hellenes enjoy the happier existence, think you, the dominant or the subject states?

[14] Or, "the outer world, the non-Hellenic races and nationalities of which we have any knowledge."
[15] Lit. "Libya."

Nay,[16] I would have you to understand (exclaimed Aristippus) that I am just as far from placing myself in the ranks of slavery; there is, I take it, a middle path between the two which it is my ambition to tread, avoiding rule and slavery alike; it lies through freedom - the high road which leads to happiness.

[16] Or, "Pardon me interrupting you, Socrates; but I have not the slightest intention of placing myself." See W. L. Newman, op. cit. i. 306.

Soc. True, if only your path could avoid human beings, as it avoids rule and slavery, there would be something in what you say. But being placed as you are amidst human beings, if you purpose neither to rule nor to be ruled, and do not mean to dance attendance, if you can help it, on those who rule, you must surely see that the stronger have an art to seat the weaker on the stool of repentance[17] both in public and in private, and to treat them as slaves. I daresay you have not failed to note this common case: a set of people has sown and planted, whereupon in comes another set and cuts their corn and fells their fruit-trees, and in every way lays siege to them because, though weaker, they refuse to pay them proper court, till at length they are persuaded to accept slavery rather than war against their betters. And in private life also, you will bear me out, the brave and powerful are known to reduce the helpless and cowardly to bondage, and to make no small profit out of their victims.

[17] See "Symp." iii. 11; "Cyrop." II. ii. 14; Plat. "Ion," 535 E; L. Dindorf ad loc.

Ar. Yes, but I must tell you I have a simple remedy against all such misadventures. I do not confine myself to any single civil community. I roam the wide world a foreigner.

Soc. Well, now, that is a masterly stroke, upon my word![18] Of course, ever since the decease of Sinis, and Sciron, and Procrustes,[19] foreign travellers have had an easy time of it. But still, if I bethink me, even in these modern days the members of free communities do pass laws in their respective countries for self- protection against wrong-doing. Over and above their personal connections, they provide themselves with a host of friends; they gird their cities about with walls and battlements; they collect armaments to ward off evil-doers; and to make security doubly sure, they furnish themselves with allies from foreign states. In spite of all which defensive machinery these same free citizens do occasionally fall victims to injustice. But you, who are without any of these aids; you, who pass half your days on the high roads where iniquity is rife;[20] you, who, into whatever city you enter, are less than the least of its free members, and moreover are just the sort of person whom any one bent on mischief would single out for attack - yet you, with your foreigner's passport, are to be exempt from injury? So you flatter yourself. And why? Will the state authorities cause proclamation to be made on your behalf: "The person of this man Aristippus is secure; let his going out and his coming in be free from danger"? Is that the ground of your confidence? or do you rather rest secure in the consciousness that you would prove such a slave as no master would care to keep? For who would care to have in his house a fellow with so slight a disposition to work and so strong a propensity to extravagance? Suppose we stop and consider that very point: how do masters deal with that sort of domestic? If I am not mistaken, they chastise his wantonness by starvation; they balk his thieving tendencies by bars and bolts where there is anything to steal; they hinder him from running away by bonds and imprisonment; they drive the sluggishness out of him with the lash. Is it not so? Or how do you proceed when you discover the like tendency in one of your domestics?

[18] Or, "Well foiled!" "A masterly fall! my prince of wrestlers."
[19] For these mythical highway robbers, see Diod. iv. 59; and for Sciron in particular, Plut. "Theseus," 10.
[20] Or, "where so many suffer wrong."

Ar. I correct them with all the plagues, till I force them to serve me properly. But, Socrates, to return to your pupil educated in the royal art,[21] which, if I mistake not, you hold to be happiness: how, may I ask, will he be better off than others who lie in evil case, in spite of themselves, simply because they suffer perforce, but in his case the hunger and the thirst, the cold shivers and the lying awake at nights, with all the changes he will ring on pain, are of his own choosing? For my part I cannot see what difference it makes, provided it is one and the same bare back which receives the stripes, whether the whipping be self-appointed or unasked for; nor indeed does it concern my body in general, provided it be my body, whether I am beleaguered by a whole armament of such evils[22] of my own will or against my will - except only for the folly which attaches to self- appointed suffering.

[21] Cf. below, IV. ii. 11; Plat. "Statesm." 259 B; "Euthyd." 291 C; K. Joel, op. cit. p. 387 foll. "Aristippus anticipates Adeimantus" ("Rep." 419), W. L. Newman, op. cit. i. 395.
[22] Cf. "suffers the slings and arrows of outrageous fortune."

Soc. What, Aristippus, does it not seem to you that, as regards such matters, there is all the difference between voluntary and involuntary suffering, in that he who starves of his own accord can eat when he chooses, and he who thirsts of his own free will can drink, and so for the rest; but he who suffers in these ways perforce cannot desist from the suffering when the humour takes him? Again, he who suffers hardship voluntarily, gaily confronts his troubles, being buoyed on hope[23] - just as a hunter in pursuit of wild beasts, through hope of capturing his quarry, finds toil a pleasure - and these are but prizes of little worth in return for their labours; but what shall we say of their reward who toil to obtain to themselves good friends, or to subdue their enemies, or that through strength of body and soul they may administer their households well, befriend their friends, and benefit the land which gave them birth? Must we not suppose that these too will take their sorrows lightly, looking to these high ends? Must we not suppose that they too will gaily confront existence, who have to support them not only their conscious virtue, but the praise and admiration of the world?[24] And once more, habits of indolence, along with the fleeting pleasures of the moment, are incapable, as gymnastic trainers say, of setting up[25] a good habit of body, or of implanting in the soul any knowledge worthy of account; whereas by painstaking endeavour in the pursuit of high and noble deeds, as good men tell us, through endurance we shall in the end attain the goal. So Hesiod somewhere says:[26]

Wickedness may a man take wholesale with ease, smooth is the way and her dwelling-place is very nigh; but in front of virtue the immortal gods have placed toil and sweat, long is the path and steep that leads to her, and rugged at the first, but when the summit of the pass is reached, then for all its roughness the path grows easy.

[23] Cf. above, I. vi. 8.
[24] Or, "in admiration of themselves, the praise and envy of the world at large."
[25] See Hippocrates, "V. Med." 18.
[26] Hesiod, "Works and Days," 285. See Plat. "Prot." 340 C; "Rep." ii. 364 D; "Laws," iv. 718 E.

And Ephicharmus[27] bears his testimony when he says:
The gods sell us all good things in return for our labours.

[27] Epicharmus of Cos, the chief comic poet among the Dorians, fl. 500 B.C. Cf. Plat. "Theaet." 152 E, "the prince of comedy"; "Gorg." 505 D.

And again in another passage he exclaims:
Set not thine heart on soft things, thou knave, lest thou light upon the hard.

And that wise man Prodicus[28] delivers himself in a like strain concerning virtue in that composition of his about Heracles, which crowds have listened to.[29] This, as far as I can recollect it, is the substance at least of what he says:

[28] Prodicus of Ceos. See Plat. "Men." 24; "Cratyl." 1; Philostr. "Vit. Soph." i. 12.
[29] Or, "which he is fond of reciting as a specimen of style." The title of the {epideixis} was {'Orai} according to Suidas, {Prodikos}.

"When Heracles was emerging from boyhood into the bloom of youth, having reached that season in which the young man, now standing upon the verge of independence, shows plainly whether he will enter upon the path of virtue or of vice, he went forth into a quiet place, and sat debating with himself which of those two paths he should pursue; and as he there sat musing, there appeared to him two women of great stature which drew nigh to him. The one was fair to look upon, frank and free by gift of nature,[30] her limbs adorned with purity and her eyes with bashfulness; sobriety set the rhythm of her gait, and she was clad in white apparel. The other was of a different type; the fleshy softness of her limbs betrayed her nurture, while the complexion of her skin was embellished that she might appear whiter and rosier than she really was, and her figure that she might seem taller than nature made her; she stared with wide-open eyes, and the raiment wherewith she was clad served but to reveal the ripeness of her bloom. With frequent glances she surveyed her person, or looked to see if others noticed her; while ever and anon she fixed her gaze upon the shadow of herself intently.

[30] Reading {eleutherion phusei, . . .} or if {eleutherion, phusei . . .} translate "nature had adorned her limbs . . ."

"Now when these two had drawn near to Heracles, she who was first named advanced at an even pace[31] towards him, but the other, in her eagerness to outstrip her, ran forward to the youth, exclaiming, 'I see you, Heracles, in doubt and difficulty what path of life to choose; make me your friend, and I will lead you to the pleasantest road and easiest. This I promise you: you shall taste all of life's sweets and escape all bitters. In the first place, you shall not trouble your brain with war or business; other topics shall engage your mind;[32] your only speculation, what meat or drink you shall find agreeable to your palate; what delight[33] of ear or eye; what pleasure of smell or touch; what darling lover's intercourse shall most enrapture you; how you shall pillow your limbs in softest slumber; how cull each individual pleasure without alloy of pain; and if ever the suspicion steal upon you that the stream of joys will one day dwindle, trust me I will not lead you where you shall replenish the store by toil of body and trouble of soul. No! others shall labour, but you shall reap the fruit of their labours; you shall withhold your hand from nought which shall bring you gain. For to all my followers I give authority and power to help themselves freely from every side.'

[31] Or, "without change in her demeanour."
[32] Reading {diese}, or {dioisei}, "you shall continue speculating solely."
[33] It will be recollected that Prodicus prided himself on {orthotes onomaton}. Possibly Xenophon is imitating (caricaturing?) his style. {terphtheies, estheies, euphrantheies}.

"Heracles hearing these words made answer: 'What, O lady, is the name you bear?' To which she: 'Know that my friends call be Happiness, but they that hate me have their own nicknames[34] for me, Vice and Naughtiness.'

[34] So the vulg. {upokorizomenoi} is interpreted. Cobet ("Pros. Xen." p. 36) suggests {upoknizomenoi} = "quippe qui desiderio pungantur."

"But just then the other of those fair women approached and spoke: 'Heracles, I too am come to you, seeing that your parents are well known to me, and in your nurture I have gauged your nature; wherefore I entertain good hope that if you choose the path which leads to me, you shall greatly bestir yourself to be the doer of many a doughty deed of noble emprise; and that I too shall be held in even higher honour for your sake, lit with the lustre shed by valorous deeds.[35] I will not cheat you with preludings of pleasure,[36] but I will relate to you the things that are according to the ordinances of God in very truth. Know then that among things that are lovely and of good report, not one have the gods bestowed upon mortal men apart from toil and pains. Would you obtain the favour of the gods, then must you pay these same gods service; would you be loved by your friends, you must benefit these friends; do you desire to be honoured by the state, you must give the state your aid; do you claim admiration for your virtue from all Hellas, you must strive to do some good to Hellas; do you wish earth to yield her fruits to you abundantly, to earth must you pay your court; do you seek to amass riches from your flocks and herds, on them must you bestow your labour; or is it your ambition to be potent as a warrior, able to save your friends and to subdue your foes, then must you learn the arts of war from those who have the knowledge, and practise their application in the field when learned; or would you e'en be powerful of limb and body, then must you habituate limbs and body to obey the mind, and exercise yourself with toil and sweat.'

[35] Or, "bathed in the splendour of thy virtues."
[36] Or, "honeyed overtures of pleasure."

"At this point, (as Prodicus relates) Vice broke in exclaiming: 'See you, Heracles, how hard and long the road is by which yonder woman would escort you to her festal joys.[37] But I will guide you by a short and easy road to happiness.'

[37] Hesiod, "Theog." 909; Milton, "L'Allegro," 12.

"Then spoke Virtue: 'Nay, wretched one, what good thing hast thou? or what sweet thing art thou acquainted with - that wilt stir neither hand nor foot to gain it? Thou, that mayest not even await the desire of pleasure, but, or ever that desire springs up, art already satiated; eating before thou hungerest, and drinking before thou thirsteth; who to eke out an appetite must invent an army of cooks and confectioners; and to whet thy thirst must lay down costliest wines, and run up and down in search of ice in summer-time; to help thy slumbers soft coverlets suffice not, but couches and feather-beds must be prepared thee and rockers to rock thee to rest; since desire for sleep in thy case springs not from toil but from vacuity and nothing in the world to do. Even the natural appetite of love thou forcest prematurely by every means thou mayest devise, confounding the sexes in thy service. Thus thou educatest thy friends: with insult in the night season and drowse of slumber during the precious hours of the day. Immortal, thou art cast forth from the company of gods, and by good men art dishonoured: that sweetest sound of all, the voice of praise, has never thrilled thine ears; and the fairest of all fair visions is hidden from thine eyes that have never beheld one bounteous deed wrought by thine own hand. If thou openest thy lips in speech, who will believe thy word? If thou hast need of aught, none shall satisfy thee. What sane man will venture to join thy rabble rout? Ill indeed are thy revellers to look upon, young men impotent of body, and old men witless in mind: in the heyday of life they batten in sleek idleness, and wearily do they drag through an age of wrinkled wretchedness: and why? they blush with shame at the thought of deeds done in the past, and groan for weariness at what is left to do. During their youth they ran riot through their sweet things, and laid up for themselves large store of bitterness against the time of eld. But my companionship is with the gods; and with the good among men my conversation; no bounteous deed, divine or human, is wrought without my aid. Therefore am I honoured in Heaven pre-eminently, and upon earth among men whose right it is to honour me;[38] as a beloved fellow-worker of all craftsmen; a faithful guardian of house and lands, whom the owners bless; a kindly helpmeet of servants;[39] a brave assistant in the labours of peace; an unflinching ally in the deeds of war; a sharer in all friendships indispensable. To my friends is given an enjoyment of meats and drinks, which is sweet in itself and devoid of trouble, in that they can endure until desire ripens, and sleep more delicious visits them than those who toil not. Yet they are not pained to part with it; nor for the sake of slumber do they let slip the performance of their duties. Among my followers the youth delights in the praises of his elders, and the old man glories in the honour of the young; with joy they call to memory their deeds of old, and in to-day's well-doing are well pleased. For my sake they are dear in the sight of God, beloved of their friends and honoured by the country of their birth. When the appointed goal is reached they lie not down in oblivion with dishonour, but bloom afresh - their praise resounded on the lips of men for ever.[40] Toils like these, O son of noble parents, Heracles, it is yours to meet with, and having endured, to enter into the heritage assured you of transcendant happiness.'"

[38] Reading {ois prosekei}, or if {proseko}, translate "to whom I am attached."
[39] Cf. "Econ." v. 8.
[40] Or, "so true is it, a branch is left them; undying honour to their name!"

This, Aristippus, in rough sketch is the theme which Prodicus pursues[41] in his "Education of

Heracles by Virtue," only he decked out his sentiments, I admit, in far more magnificant phrases than I have ventured on. Were it not well, Aristippus, to lay to heart these sayings, and to strive to bethink you somewhat of that which touches the future of our life?

[41] Reading {diokei}, al. {diokei} = "so Prodicus arranged the parts of his discourse."

II

At another time, he had noticed the angry temper shown by Lamprocles, the elder of his sons, towards their mother, and thus addressed himself to the lad.

Soc. Pray, my son, did you ever hear of certain people being called ungrateful?

That I have (replied the young man).

Soc. And have you understood what it is they do to get that bad name?

Lamp. Yes, I have: when any one has been kindly treated, and has it in his power to requite the kindness but neglects to do so, men call him ungrateful.

Soc. And you admit that people reckon the ungrateful among wrongdoers?

Lamp. I do.

Soc. And has it ever struck you to inquire whether, as regards the right or wrong of it, ingratitude may not perhaps resemble some such conduct as the enslavement, say, of prisoners, which is accounted wrong towards friends but justifiable towards enemies?

Lamp. Yes, I have put that question to myself. In my opinion, no matter who confers the kindness, friend or foe, the recipient should endeavour to requite it, failing which he is a wrongdoer.

Soc. Then if that is how the matter stands, ingratitude would be an instance of pure unadulterate wrongdoing?

Lamprocles assented to the proposition.

Soc. It follows, then, that in proportion to the greatness of the benefit conferred, the greater his misdoing who fails to requite the kindness?

Lamprocles again assented.

Socrates continued: And where can we hope to find greater benefits than those which children derive from their parents - their father and mother who brought them out of nothingness into being, who granted them to look upon all these fair sights, and to partake of all those blessings which the gods bestow on man, things so priceless in our eyes that one and all we shudder at the thought of leaving them, and states have made death the penalty for the greatest crimes, because there is no greater evil through fear of which to stay iniquity.

You do not suppose that human beings produce children for the sake of carnal pleasure[1] merely; were this the motive, street and bordell are full of means to quit them of that thrall; whereas nothing is plainer than the pains we take to seek out wives who shall bear us the finest children.[2] With these we wed, and carry on the race. The man has a twofold duty to perform: partly in cherishing her who is to raise up children along with him, and partly towards the children yet unborn in providing them with things that he thinks will contribute to their well-being - and of these as large a store as possible. The woman, conceiving, bears her precious burthen with travail and pain, and at the risk of life itself - sharing with that within her womb the food on which she herself is fed. And when with much labour she has borne to the end and brought forth her offspring, she feeds it and watches over it with tender care - not in return for any good thing previously received, for indeed the babe itself is little conscious of its benefactor and cannot even signify its wants; only she, the mother, making conjecture of what is good for it, and what will please it, essays to satisfy it;[3] and for many months she feeds it night and day, enduring the toil nor recking what return she shall receive for all her trouble. Nor does the care and kindness of parents end with nurture; but when the children seem of an age to learn, they teach them themselves whatever cunning they possess, as a guide to life, or where they feel that another is more competent, to him they send them to be taught at their expense. Thus they watch over their children, doing all in their power to enable them to grow up to be as good as possible.

[1] Lit. "the joys of Aphrodite."
[2] "For the procreation of children." See below, IV. iv. 22; "Pol. Lac." i.
[3] Lit. "to leave nought lacking."

So be it (the youth answered); but even if she have done all that, and twenty times as much, no soul on earth could endure my mother's cross- grained temper.

Then Socrates: Which, think you, would be harder to bear - a wild beast's savagery or a mother's?

Lamp. To my mind, a mother's - at least if she be such as mine.

Soc. Dear me! And has this mother ever done you any injury - such as people frequently receive from beasts, by bite or kick?

Lamp. If she has not done quite that, she uses words which any one would sooner sell his life than listen to.

Soc. And how many annoyances have you caused your mother, do you suppose, by fretfulness and peevishness in word and deed, night and day, since you were a little boy? How much sorrow and pain, when you were ill?

Lamp. Well, I never said or did anything to bring a blush to her cheeks.

Soc. No, come now! Do you suppose it is harder for you to listen to your mother's speeches than for actor to listen to actor on the tragic stage,[4] when the floodgates of abuse are opened?

[4] See Grote, "H. G." viii. 457; Plut. "Solon," xxix.

Lamp. Yes; for the simple reason that they know it is all talk on their parts. The inquisitor may cross-question, but he will not inflict a fine; the threatener may hurl his menaces, but he will do no mischief - that is why they take it all so easily.

Soc. Then ought you to fly into a passion, who know well enough that, whatever your mother says, she is so far from meaning you mischief that she is actually wishing blessings to descend upon you beyond all others? Or do you believe that your mother is really ill disposed towards you?

Lamp. No, I do not think that.

Soc. Then this mother, who is kindly disposed to you, and takes such tender care of you when you are ill to make you well again, and to see that you want for nothing which may help you; and, more than all, who is perpetually pleading for blessings in your behalf and offering her vows to Heaven[5] - can you say of her that she is cross-grained and harsh? For my part, I think, if you cannot away with such a mother, you cannot away with such blessings either.

[5] Or, "paying vows."

But tell me (he proceeded), do you owe service to any living being, think you? or are you prepared to stand alone? Prepared not to please or try to please a single soul? to follow none? To obey neither general nor ruler of any sort? Is that your attitude, or do you admit that you owe allegience to somebody?

Lamp. Yes; certainly I owe allegiance.

Soc. May I take it that you are willing to please at any rate your neighbour, so that he may kindle a fire for you in your need, may prove himself a ready helpmate in good fortune, or if you chance on evil and are stumbling, may friendlily stand by your side to aid?

Lamp. I am willing.

Soc. Well, and what of that other chance companion - your fellow- traveller by land or sea? what of any others, you may light upon? is it indifferent to you whether these be friends or not, or do you admit that the goodwill of these is worth securing by some pains on your part?

Lamp. I do.

Soc. It stands thus then: you are prepared to pay attention to this, that, and the other stranger, but to your mother who loves you more than all else, you are bound to render no service, no allegiance? Do you not know that whilst the state does not concern itself with ordinary ingratitude or pass judicial sentence on it; whilst it overlooks the thanklessness of those who fail to make return for kindly treatment, it reserves its pains and penalties for the special case? If a man render not the service and allegiance due to his parents, on him the finger of the law is laid; his name is struck off the roll; he is forbidden to hold the archonship - which is as much as to say, "Sacrifices in behalf of the state offered by such a man would be no offerings, being tainted with impiety; nor could aught else be 'well and justly' performed of which he is the doer." Heaven help us! If a man fail to adorn the sepulchre of his dead parents the state takes cognisance of the matter, and inquisition is made in the scrutiny of the magistrates.[6] And as for you, my son, if you are in your sober senses, you will earnestly entreat your mother, lest the very gods take you to be an ungrateful being, and on their side also refuse to do you good; and you will beware of men also, lest they should perceive your neglect of your parents, and with one consent hold you in dishonour;[7] and so you find yourself in a desert devoid of friends. For if once the notion be entertained that here is a man ungrateful to his parents, no one will believe that any kindness shown you would be other than thrown away.

[6] Lit. "the docimasia." See Gow, "Companion," xiv.
[7] "Visiti with atimia."

III

At another time the differences between two brothers named Chaerephon and Chaerecrates, both well known to him, had drawn his attention; and on seeing the younger of the two he thus addressed him.

Soc. Tell me, Chaerecrates, you are not, I take it, one of those strange people who believe that goods are better and more precious than a brother;[1] and that too although the former are but senseless chattels which need protection, the latter a sensitive and sensible being who can afford it; and what is more, he is himself alone, whilst as for them their name is legion. And here again is a marvellous thing: that a man should count his brother a loss, because the goods of his brother are not his; but he does not count his fellow-citizens loss, and yet their possessions are not his; only it seems in their case he has wits to see that to dwell securely with many and have enough is better than to own the whole wealth of a community and to live in dangerous isolation; but this same doctrine as applied to brothers they ignore. Again, if a man have the means, he will purchase domestic slaves, because he wants assistants in his work; he will acquire friends, because he needs their support; but this brother of his - who cares about brothers? It seems a friend may be discovered in an ordinary citizen, but not in a blood relation who is also a brother. And yet it is a great vantage-ground towards friendship to have sprung from the same loins and to have been suckled at the same breasts, since even among beasts a certain natural craving, and sympathy springs up between creatures reared together.[2] Added to which, a man who has brothers commands more respect from the rest of the world than the man who has none, and who must fight his own battles.[3]

[1] Cf. "Merchant of Venice," II. viii. 17: "Justice! the law! my ducats, and my daughter!"
[2] Or, "a yearning after their foster-brothers manifests itself in animals." See "Cyrop." VIII. vii. 14 foll. for a parallel to this discussion.
[3] Lit. "and is less liable to hostility."

Chaer. I daresay, Socrates, where the differences are not profound, reason would a man should bear with his brother, and not avoid him for some mere trifle's sake, for a brother of the right sort is, as you say, a blessing; but if he be the very antithesis of that, why should a man lay his hand to achieve the impossible?

Soc. Well now, tell me, is there nobody whom Chaerephon can please any more than he can please yourself; or do some people find him agreeable enough?

Chaer. Nay, there you hit it. That is just why I have a right to detest him. He can be pleasing enough to others, but to me, whenever he appears on the scene, he is not a blessing - no! but by every manner of means the reverse.

Soc. May it not happen that just as a horse is no gain to the inexpert rider who essays to handle him, so in like manner, if a man tries to deal with his brother after an ignorant fashion, this same brother will kick?

Chaer. But is it likely now? How should I be ignorant of the art of dealing with my brother if I know the art of repaying kind words and good deeds in kind? But a man who tries all he can to annoy me by word and deed, I can neither bless nor benefit, and, what is more, I will not try.

Soc. Well now, that is a marvellous statement, Chaerecrates. Your dog, the serviceable guardian of your flocks, who will fawn and lick the hand of your shepherd, when you come near him can only growl and show his teeth. Well; you take no notice of the dog's ill-temper, you try to propitiate him by kindness; but your brother? If your brother were what he ought to be, he would be a great blessing to you - that you admit; and, as you further confess, you know the secret of kind acts and words, yet you will not set yourself to apply means to make him your best of friends.

Chaer. I am afraid, Socrates, that I have no wisdom or cunning to make Chaerephon bear himself towards me as he should.

Soc. Yet there is no need to apply any recondite or novel machinery. Only bait your hook in the way best known to yourself, and you will capture him; whereupon he will become your devoted friend.

Chaer. If you are aware that I know some love-charm, Socrates, of which I am the happy but unconscious possessor, pray make haste and enlighten me.

Soc. Answer me then. Suppose you wanted to get some acquaintance to invite you to dinner when he next keeps holy day,[4] what steps would you take?

[4] "When he next does sacrifice"; see "Hiero," viii. 3. Cf. Theophr. "Char." xv. 2, and Prof. Jebb's note ad loc.

Chaer. No doubt I should set him a good example by inviting him myself on a like occasion.

Soc. And if you wanted to induce some friend to look after your affairs during your absence abroad, how would you achieve your purpose?

Chaer. No doubt I should present a precedent in undertaking to look after his in like circumstances.

Soc. And if you wished to get some foreign friend to take you under his roof while visiting his country, what would you do?

Chaer. No doubt I should begin by offering him the shelter of my own roof when he came to Athens, in order to enlist his zeal in furthering the objects of my visit; it is plain I should first show my readiness to do as much for him in a like case.

Soc. Why, it seems you are an adept after all in all the philtres known to man, only you chose to conceal your knowledge all the while; or is it that you shrink from taking the first step because of the scandal you will cause by kindly advances to your brother? And yet it is commonly held to redound to a man's praise to have outstripped an enemy in mischief or a friend in kindness. Now if it seemed to me that Chaerephon were better fitted to lead the way towards this friendship,[5] I should have tried to persuade him to take the first step in winning your affection, but now I am persuaded the first move belongs to you, and to you the final victory.

[5] Reading {pros ten philian}, or if {phusin}, transl. "natural disposition."

Chaer. A startling announcement, Socrates, from your lips, and most unlike you, to bid me the younger take precedence of my elder brother. Why, it is contrary to the universal custom of mankind, who look to the elder to take the lead in everything, whether as a speaker or an actor.

Soc. How so? Is it not the custom everywhere for the younger to step aside when he meets his elder in the street and to give him place? Is he not expected to get up and offer him his seat, to pay him the honour of a soft couch,[6] to yield him precedence in argument?

[6] Lit. "with a soft bed," or, as we say, "the best bedroom."

My good fellow, do not stand shilly-shallying,[7] but put out your hand caressingly, and you will see the worthy soul will respond at once with alacrity. Do you not note your brother's character, proud and frank and sensitive to honour? He is not a mean and sorry rascal to be caught by a bribe - no better way indeed for such riff-raff. No! gentle natures need a finer treatment. You can best hope to work on them by affection.

[7] Or, "have no fears, essay a soothing treatment."

Chaer. But suppose I do, and suppose that, for all my attempts, he shows no change for the better?

Soc. At the worst you will have shown yourself to be a good, honest, brotherly man, and he will appear as a sorry creature on whom kindness is wasted. But nothing of the sort is going to happen, as I conjecture. My belief is that as soon as he hears your challenge, he will embrace the contest; pricked on by emulous pride, he will insist upon getting the better of you in kindness of word and deed.

At present you two are in the condition of two hands formed by God to help each other, but which have let go their business and have turned to hindering one another all they can. You are a pair of feet fashioned on the Divine plan to work together, but which have neglected this in order to trammel each other's gait. Now is it not insensate stupidity[8] to use for injury what was meant for advantage? And yet in fashioning two brothers God intends them, methinks, to be of more benefit to one another than either two hands, or two feet, or two eyes, or any other of those pairs which belong to man from his birth.[9] Consider how powerless these hands of ours if called upon to combine their action at two points more than a single fathom's length apart;[10] and these feet could not stretch asunder[11] even a bare fathom; and these eyes, for all the wide-reaching range we claim for them, are incapable of seeing simultaneously the back and front of an object at even closer quarters. But a pair of brothers, linked in bonds of amity, can work each for the other's good, though seas divide them.[12]

[8] "Boorishness verging upon monomania."
[9] "With which man is endowed at birth."
[10] "More than an 'arms'-stretch' asunder."
[11] Lit. "reach at one stretch two objects, even over that small distance."
[12] "Though leagues separate them."

IV

I have at another time heard him discourse on the kindred theme of friendship in language well calculated, as it seemed to me, to help a man to choose and also to use his friends aright.

He (Socrates) had often heard the remark made that of all possessions there is none equal to that of a good and sincere friend; but, in spite of this assertion, the mass of people, as far as he could see, concerned themselves about nothing so little as the acquisition of friends. Houses, and fields, and slaves, and cattle, and furniture of all sorts (he said) they were at pains to acquire, and they strove hard to keep what they had got; but to procure for themselves this greatest of all blessings, as they admitted a friend to be, or to keep the friends whom they already possessed, not one man in a hundred ever gave himself a thought. It was noticeable, in the case of a sickness befalling a man's friend and one of his own household simultaneously, the promptness with which the master would fetch the doctor to his domestic, and take every precaution necessary for his recovery, with much expenditure of pains; but meanwhile little account would be taken of the friend in like condition, and if both should die, he will show signs of deep annoyance at the death of his domestic, which, as he reflects, is a positive loss to him; but as regards his friend his position is in no wise materially affected, and thus, though he would never dream of leaving his other possessions disregarded and ill cared for, friendship's mute appeal is met with flat indifference.[1]

[1] Or, "the cry of a friend for careful tending falls on deaf ears."

Or to take (said he) a crowning instance:[2] with regard to ordinary possessions, however multifarious these may be, most people are at least acquainted with their number, but if you ask a man to enumerate his friends, who are not so very many after all perhaps, he cannot; or if, to oblige the inquirer, he essays to make a list, he will presently retract the names of some whom he had previously included.[3] Such is the amount of thought which people bestow upon their friends.

[2] Or, "Nor had he failed to observe another striking contrast." Cf. Cic. "Lael." 17; Diog. Laert. ii. 30.
[3] i.e. "like a chess-player recalling a move."

And yet what thing else may a man call his own is comparable to this one best possession! what rather will not serve by contrast to enhance the value of an honest friend! Think of a horse or a yoke of oxen; they have their worth; but who shall gauge the worth of a worthy friend? Kindlier and more constant than the faithfullest of slaves - this is that possession best named all-serviceable.[4] Consider what the post is that he assigns himself! to meet and supplement what is lacking to the welfare of his friends, to promote their private and their public interests, is his concern. Is there need of kindly action in any quarter? he will throw in the full weight of his support. Does some terror confound? he is at hand to help and defend by expenditure of money and of energy,[5] by appeals to reason or resort to force. His the privilege alike to gladden the prosperous in the hour of success and to sustain their footing who have well-nigh slipped. All that the hands of a man may minister, all that the eyes of each are swift to see, the ears to hear, and the feet to compass, he with his helpful arts will not fall short of. Nay, not seldom that which a man has failed to accomplish for himself, has missed seeing or hearing or attaining, a friend acting in behalf of friend will achieve vicariously. And yet, albeit to try and tend a tree for the sake of its fruit is not uncommon, this copious mine of wealth - this friend - attracts only a lazy and listless attention on the part of more than half the world.

[4] "A vessel fit for all work indeed is this friend." Cf. Ar. "Ach." 936, {pagkhreston aggos estai}, like the "leather bottel."
[5] Or, "by dint of his diplomacy."

V

I remember listening to another argument of his, the effect of which would be to promote self-examination. The listener must needs be brought to ask himself, "Of what worth am I to my friends?" It happened thus. One of those who were with him was neglectful, as he noted, of a friend who was at the pinch of poverty (Antisthenes).[1] Accordingly, in the presence of the negligent person and of several others, he proceeded to question the sufferer.

[1] *Antisthenes, "cynicorum et stoicorum parens." Cic. "de Or." iii. 17; "ad Att." xii. 38. See below, III. iii. 17; "Symp." passim; Diog. Laert. II. v.; VI. i.*

Soc. What say you, Antisthenes? - have friends their values like domestic slaves? One of these latter may be worth perhaps two minae,[2] another only half a mina, a third five, and a fourth as much as ten; while they do say that Nicias,[3] the son of Niceratus, paid a whole talent for a superintendent of his silver mines. And so I propound the question to myself as follows: "Have friends, like slaves, their market values?"

[2] *A mina = L4 circ.*
[3] *For Nicias see Thuc. vii. 77 foll.; "Revenues," iv. 14; Plut. "Nic." IV. v.; Lys. "de bon. Aristoph." 648.*

Not a doubt of it (replied Antisthenes). At any rate, I know that I would rather have such a one as my friend than be paid two minae, and there is such another whose worth I would not estimate at half a mina, and a third with whom I would not part for ten, and then again a fourth whose friendship would be cheap if it cost me all the wealth and pains in the world to purchase it.

Well then (continued Socrates), if that be so, would it not be well if every one were to examine himself: "What after all may I chance to be worth to my friends?" Should he not try to become as dear as possible, so that his friends will not care to give him up? How often do I hear the complaint: "My friend So-and-so has given me up"; or "Such an one, whom I looked upon as a friend, has sacrificed me for a mina." And every time I hear these remarks, the question arises in my mind: If the vendor of a worthless slave is ready to part with him to a purchaser for what he will fetch - is there not at least a strong temptation to part with a base friend when you have a chance of making something on the exchange? Good slaves, as far as I can see, are not so knocked down to the hammer; no, nor good friends so lightly parted with.

VI

Again, in reference to the test to be applied, if we would gauge the qualifications of a friend worth the winning, the following remarks of Socrates could not fail, I think, to prove instructive.[1]

[1] *Or, "Again, as to establishing a test of character, since a friend worth having must be of a particular type, I cannot but think that the following remarks would prove instructive."*

Tell me (said Socrates, addressing Critobulus), supposing we stood in need of a good friend, how should we set about his discovery? We must, in the first place, I suppose, seek out one who is master of his appetites, not under the dominion, that is, of his belly, not addicted to the wine-cup or to lechery or sleep or idleness, since no one enslaved to such tyrants could hope to do his duty either by himself or by his friends, could he?

Certainly not (Critobulus answered).

Soc. Do you agree, then, that we must hold aloof from every one so dominated?

Cri. Most assuredly.

Well then (proceeded Socrates), what shall we say of the spendthrift who has lost his independence and is for ever begging of his neighbours; if he gets anything out of them he cannot repay, but if he fails to get anything, he hates you for not giving - do you not think that this man too would prove but a disagreeable friend?

Cri. Certainly.

Soc. Then we must keep away from him too?

Cri. That we must.

Soc. Well! and what of the man whose strength lies in monetary transactions?[2] His one craving is to amass money; and for that reason he is an adept at driving a hard bargain[3] - glad enough to take in, but loath to pay out.

[2] Or, "the money-lender? He has a passion for big money-bags."
[3] Or, "hard in all his dealings."

Cri. In my opinion he will prove even a worse fellow than the last.

Soc. Well! and what of that other whose passion for money-making is so absorbing that he has no leisure for anything else, save how he may add to his gains?

Cri. Hold aloof from him, say I, since there is no good to be got out of him or his society.

Soc. Well! what of the quarrelsome and factious person[4] whose main object is to saddle his friends with a host of enemies?

[4] "The partisan."

Cri. For God's sake let us avoid him also.

Soc. But now we will imagine a man exempt indeed from all the above defects - a man who has no objection to receive kindnesses, but it never enters into his head to do a kindness in return.

Cri. There will be no good in him either. But, Socrates, what kind of man shall we endeavour to make our friend? what is he like?

Soc. I should say he must be just the converse of the above: he has control over the pleasures of the body, he is kindly disposed,[5] upright in all his dealings,[6] very zealous is he not to be outdone in kindness by his benefactors, if only his friends may derive some profit from his acquaintance.

[5] Reading {eunous}, or if {euorkos}, transl. "a man of his word."
[6] Or, "easy to deal with."

Cri. But how are we to test these qualities, Socrates, before acquaintance?

Soc. How do we test the merits of a sculptor? - not by inferences drawn from the talk of the artist merely. No, we look to what he has already achieved. These former statues of his were nobly executed, and we trust he will do equally well with the rest.

Cri. You mean that if we find a man whose kindness to older friends is established, we may take it as proved that he will treat his newer friends as amiably?

Soc. Why, certainly, if I see a man who has shown skill in the handling of horses previously, I argue that he will handle others no less skilfully again.

Cri. Good! and when we have discovered a man whose friendship is worth having, how ought we to make him our friend?

Soc. First we ought to ascertain the will of Heaven whether it be advisable to make him our friend.

Cri. Well! and how are we to effect the capture of this friend of our choice, whom the gods approve? will you tell me that?

Not, in good sooth (replied Socrates), by running him down like a hare, nor by decoying him like a bird, or by force like a wild boar.[7] To capture a friend against his will is a toilsome business, and to bind him in fetters like a slave by no means easy. Those who are so treated are apt to become foes instead of friends.[8]

[7] *Reading {kaproi}, al. {ekhthroi}, "an enemy."*
[8] *Or, "Hate rather than friendship is the outcome of these methods."*

Cri. But how convert them into friends?

Soc. There are certain incantations, we are told, which those who know them have only to utter, and they can make friends of whom they list; and there are certain philtres also which those who have the secret of them may administer to whom they like and win their love.

Cri. From what source shall we learn them?

Soc. You need not go farther than Homer to learn that which the Sirens sang to Odysseus,[9] the first words of which run, I think, as follows:

Hither, come hither, thou famous man, Odysseus, great glory of the Achaeans!

[9] *"Od." xii. 184.*

Cri. And did the magic words of this spell serve for all men alike? Had the Sirens only to utter this one incantation, and was every listener constrained to stay?

Soc. No; this was the incantation reserved for souls athirst for fame, of virtue emulous.

Cri. Which is as much as to say, we must suit the incantation to the listener, so that when he hears the words he shall not think that the enchanter is laughing at him in his sleeve. I cannot certainly conceive a method better calculated to excite hatred and repulsion than to go to some one who knows that he is small and ugly and a weakling, and to breathe in his ears the flattering tale that he is beautiful and tall and stalwart. But do you know any other love- charms, Socrates?

Soc. I cannot say that I do; but I have heard that Pericles[10] was skilled in not a few, which he poured into the ear of our city and won her love.

[10] *See above, I. ii. 40; "Symp." viii. 39.*

Cri. And how did Themistocles[11] win our city's love?

[11] *See below, III. vi. 2; IV. ii. 2.*

Soc. Ah, that was not by incantation at all. What he did was to encircle our city with an amulet of saving virtue.[12]

[12] *See Herod. vii. 143, "the wooden wall"; Thuc. i. 93, "'the walls' of Athens."*

Cri. You would imply, Socrates, would you not, that if we want to win the love of any good man we need to be good ourselves in speech and action?

And did you imagine (replied Socrates) that it was possible for a bad man to make good friends?

Cri. Why, I could fancy I had seen some sorry speech-monger who was fast friends with a great and noble statesman; or again, some born commander and general who was boon companion with fellows quite incapable of generalship.[13]

[13] *Or, "Why, yes, when I see some base orator fast friends with a great leader of the people; or, again, some fellow incapable of generalship a comrade to the greatest captains of his age."*

Soc. But in reference to the point we were discussing, may I ask whether you know of any one who can attach a useful friend to himself without being of use in return?[14] Can service ally in friendship with disservice?

[14] Add, "Can service ally in friendship with disservice? Must there not be a reciprocity of service to make friendship lasting?"

Cri. In good sooth no. But now, granted it is impossible for a base man to be friends with the beautiful and noble,[14b] I am concerned at once to discover if one who is himself of a beautiful and noble character can, with a wave of the hand, as it were, attach himself in friendship to every other beautiful and noble nature.

[14b] {kalous kagathous}.

Soc. What perplexes and confounds you, Critobulus, is the fact that so often men of noble conduct, with souls aloof from baseness, are not friends but rather at strife and discord with one another, and deal more harshly by one another than they would by the most good-for- nothing of mankind.

Cri. Yes, and this holds true not of private persons only, but states, the most eager to pursue a noble policy and to repudiate a base one, are frequently in hostile relation to one another. As I reason on these things my heart fails me, and the question, how friends are to be acquired, fills me with despondency. The bad, as I see, cannot be friends with one another. For how can such people, the ungrateful, or reckless, or covetous, or faithless, or incontinent, adhere together as friends? Without hesitation I set down the bad as born to be foes not friends, and as bearing the birthmark of internecine hate. But then again, as you suggest, no more can these same people harmonise in friendship with the good. For how should they who do evil be friends with those who hate all evil-doing? And if, last of all, they that cultivate virtue are torn by party strife in their struggle for the headship of the states, envying one another, hating one another, who are left to be friends? where shall goodwill and faithfulness be found among men?

Soc. The fact is there is some subtlety in the texture of these things.[15] Seeds of love are implanted in man by nature. Men have need of one another, feel pity, help each other by united efforts, and in recognition of the fact show mutual gratitude. But there are seeds of war implanted also. The same objects being regarded as beautiful or agreeable by all alike, they do battle for their possession; a spirit of disunion[16] enters, and the parties range themselves in adverse camps. Discord and anger sound a note of war: the passion of more- having, staunchless avarice, threatens hostility; and envy is a hateful fiend.[17]

[15] i.e. a cunning intertwining of the threads of warp and woof.
[16] Cf. Shelley, "The devil of disunion in their souls."
[17] The diction is poetical.

But nevertheless, through all opposing barriers friendship steals her way and binds together the beautiful and good among mankind.[18] Such is their virtue that they would rather possess scant means painlessly than wield an empire won by war. In spite of hunger and thirst they will share their meat and drink without a pang. Not bloom of lusty youth, nor love's delights can warp their self-control; nor will they be tempted to cause pain where pain should be unknown. It is theirs not merely to eschew all greed of riches, not merely to make a just and lawful distribution of wealth, but to supply what is lacking to the needs of one another. Theirs it is to compose strife and discord not in painless oblivion simply, but to the general advantage. Theirs also to hinder such extravagance of anger as shall entail remorse hereafter. And as to envy they will make a clean sweep and clearance of it: the good things which a man possesses shall be also the property of his friends, and the goods which they possess are to be looked upon as his. Where then is the improbability that the beautiful and noble should be sharers in the honours[19] of the state not only without injury, but even to their mutual advantage?

[18] Or, as we say, "the elite of human kind."
[19] "And the offices."

They indeed who covet and desire the honours and offices in a state for the sake of the liberty thereby given them to embezzle the public moneys, to deal violently by their fellow-creatures, and to batten in luxury themselves, may well be regarded as unjust and villainous persons incapable of harmony with one another. But if a man desire to obtain these selfsame honours in order that, being himself secure against wrong-doing, he may be able to assist his friends in what is right, and, raised to a high position, [20] may essay to confer some blessing on the land of his fathers, what is there to hinder him from working in harmony with some other of a like spirit? Will he, with the "beautiful and noble" at his side, be less able to aid his friends? or will his power to benfit the community be shortened because the flower of that community are fellow-workers in that work? Why, even in the contests of the games it is obvious that if it were possible for the stoutest combatants to combine against the weakest, the chosen band would come off victors in every bout, and would carry off all the prizes. This indeed is against the rules of the actual arena; but in the field of politics, where the beautiful and good hold empery, and there is nought to hinder any from combining with whomsoever a man may choose to benefit the state, it will be a clear gain, will it not, for any one engaged in state affairs to make the best men his friends, whereby he will find partners and co-operators in his aims instead of rivals and antagonists? And this at least is obvious: in case of foreign war a man will need allies, but all the more if in the ranks opposed to him should stand the flower of the enemy.[21] Moreover, those who are willing to fight your battles must be kindly dealt with, that goodwill may quicken to enthusiasm; and one good man[22] is better worth your benefiting that a dozen knaves, since a little kindness goes a long way with the good, but with the base the more you give them the more they ask for.

[20] "As archon," or "raised to rule."
[21] Lit. "the beautiful and good."
[22] Or, "the best, though few, are better worth your benefiting than the many base."

So keep a good heart, Critobulus; only try to become good yourself, and when you have attained, set to your hand to capture the beautiful and good. Perhaps I may be able to give you some help in this quest, being myself an adept in Love's lore.[23] No matter who it is for whom my heart is aflame; in an instant my whole soul is eager to leap forth. With vehemence I speed to the mark. I, who love, demand to be loved again; this desire in me must be met by counter desire in him; this thirst for his society by thirst reciprocal for mine. And these will be your needs also, I foresee, whenever you are seized with longing to contract a friendship. Do not hide from me, therefore, whom you would choose as a friend, since, owing to the pains I take to please him who pleases me, I am not altogether unversed, I fancy, in the art of catching men.[24]

[23] "An authority in matters of love." Cf. Plat. "Symp." 177 D; Xen. "Symp." viii. 2.
[24] See below, III. xi. 7; cf. Plat. "Soph." 222; N. T. Matt. iv. 19, {alieis anthropon}.

Critobulus replied: Why, these are the very lessons of instruction, Socrates, for which I have been long athirst, and the more particularly if this same love's lore will enable me to capture those who are good of soul and those who are beautiful of person.

Soc. Nay, now I warn you, Critobulus, it is not within the province of my science to make the beautiful endure him who would lay hands upon them. And that is why men fled from Scylla, I am persuaded, because she laid hands upon them; but the Sirens were different - they laid hands on nobody, but sat afar off and chanted their spells in the ears of all; and therefore, it is said, all men endured to listen, and were charmed.

Cri. I promise I will not lay violent hands on any; therefore, if you have any good device for winning friends, instruct your pupil.

Soc. And if there is to be no laying on of the hands, there must be no application either of the lips; is it agreed?

Cri. No, nor application of the lips to any one - not beautiful.

Soc. See now! you cannot open your mouth without some luckless utterence. Beauty suffers no such liberty, however eagerly the ugly may invite it, making believe some quality of soul must rank them with the beautiful.

Cri. Be of good cheer then; let the compact stand thus: "Kisses for the beautiful, and for the good a rain of kisses." So now teach us the art of catching friends.

Soc. Well then, when you wish to win some one's affection, you will allow me to lodge information against you to the effect that you admire him and desire to be his friend?

Cri. Lodge the indictment, with all my heart. I never heard of any one who hated his admirers.

Soc. And if I add to the indictment the further charge that through your admiration you are kindly disposed towards him, you will not feel I am taking away your character?

Cri. Why, no; for myself I know a kindly feeling springs up in my heart towards any one whom I conceive to be kindly disposed to me.

Soc. All this I shall feel empowered to say about you to those whose friendship you seek, and I can promise further help; only there is a comprehensive "if" to be considered: if you will further authorise me to say that you are devoted to your friends; that nothing gives you so much joy as a good friend; that you pride yourself no less on the fine deeds of those you love than on your own; and on their good things equally with your own; that you never weary of plotting and planning to procure them a rich harvest of the same; and lastly, that you have discovered a man's virtue is to excel his friends in kindness and his foes in hostility. If I am authorised thus to report of you, I think you will find me a serviceable fellow-hunter in the quest of friends, which is the conquest of the good.

Cri. Why this appeal to me? - as if you had not free permission to say exactly what you like about me.

Soc. No; that I deny, on the authority of Aspasia.[25] I have it from her own lips. "Good matchmakers," she said tome, "were clever hands at cementing alliances between people, provided the good qualities they vouched for were truthfully reported; but when it came to their telling lies, for her part she could not compliment them.[26] Their poor deluded dupes ended by hating each other and the go-betweens as well." Now I myself am so fully persuaded of the truth of this that I feel it is not in my power to say aught in your praise which I cannot say with truth.

[25] *Aspasia, daughter of Axiochus, of Miletus. See "Econ." iii. 14; Plat. "Menex." 235 E; Aesch. Socrat. ap. Cic. "de Invent." I. xxxi. 51. See Grote, "H. G." vi. 132 foll.; Cobet, "Pros. Xen."*

[26] *Reading {ouk ethelein epainein}, or if {ouk ophelein epainousas} with Kuhner transl. "Good matchmakers, she told me, have to consult truth when reporting favourably of any one: then indeed they are terribly clever at bringing people together: whereas false flatterers do no good; their dupes," etc.*

Cri. Really, Socrates, you are a wonderfully good friend to me - in so far as I have any merit which will entitle me to win a friend, you will lend me a helping hand, it seems; otherwise you would rather not forge any petty fiction for my benefit.

Soc. But tell me, how shall I assist you best, think you? By praising you falsely or by persuading you to try to be a good man? Or if it is not plain to you thus, look at the matter by the light of some examples. I wish to introduce you to a shipowner, or to make him your friend: I begin by singing your praises to him falsely thus, "You will find him a good pilot"; he catches at the phrase, and entrusts his ship to you, who have no notion of guiding a vessel. What can you expect but to make shipwreck of the craft and yourself together? or suppose by similar false assertions I can persuade the state at large to entrust her destinies to you - "a man with a fine genius for command," I say, "a practised lawyer," "a politician born," and so forth. The odds are, the state and you may come to grief through you. Or to take an instance from everyday life. By my falsehoods I persuade some private person to entrust his affairs to you as "a really careful and business-like person with a head for economy." When put to the test would not your administration prove ruinous, and the figure you cut ridiculous? No, my dear friend, there is but one road, the shortest, safest, best, and it is simply this: In whatsoever you desire to be deemed good, endeavour to be good. For of all the virtues namable among men, consider, and you will find there is not one but may be increased by learning and practice. For my part then, Critobulus, these are the principles on which we ought to go a- hunting; but if you take a different view, I am all attention, please instruct me.

Then Critobulus: Nay, Socrates, I should be ashamed to gainsay what you have said; if I did, it would neither be a noble statement nor a true.[27]

[27] {kala . . . alethe}.

VII

He had two ways of dealing with the difficulties of his friends: where ignorance was the cause, he tried to meet the trouble by a dose of common sense; or where want and poverty were to blame, by lessoning them that they should assist one another according to their ability; and here I may mention certain incidents which occurred within my own knowledge. How, for instance, he chanced upon Aristarchus wearing the look of one who suffered from a fit of the "sullens," and thus accosted him.

Soc. You seem to have some trouble on your mind, Aristarchus; if so, you should share it with your friends. Perhaps together we might lighten the weight of it a little.

Aristarchus answered: Yes, Socrates, I am in sore straits indeed. Ever since the party strife declared itself in the city,[1] what with the rush of people to Piraeus, and the wholesale banishments, I have been fairly at the mercy of my poor deserted female relatives. Sisters, nieces, cousins, they have all come flocking to me for protection. I have fourteen free-born souls, I tell you, under my single roof, and how are we to live? We can get nothing out of the soil - that is in the hands of the enemy; nothing from my house property, for there is scarcely a living soul left in the city; my furniture? no one will buy it; money? there is none to be borrowed - you would have a better chance to find it by looking for it on the road than to borrow it from a banker. Yes, Socrates, to stand by and see one's relatives die of hunger is hard indeed, and yet to feed so many at such a pinch impossible.

[1] i.e. circa 404-403 B.C. See "Hell." II. iv.

After he listened to the story, Socrates asked: How comes it that Ceramon,[2] with so many mouths to feed, not only contrives to furnish himself and them with the necessaries of life, but to realise a handsome surplus, whilst you being in like plight[3] are afraid you will one and all perish of starvation for want of the necessaries of life?

[2] An employer of labour, apparently, on a grand scale.
[3] Lit. "with your large family to feed." L. Dindorf would like to read {su de oligous}, "you with your small family."

Ar. Why, bless your soul, do you not see he has only slaves and I have free-born souls to feed?
Soc. And which should you say were the better human beings, the free- born members of your household or Ceramon's slaves?
Ar. The free souls under my roof without a doubt.

Soc. Is it not a shame, then, that he with his baser folk to back him should be in easy circumstances, while you and your far superior household are in difficulties?

Ar. To be sure it is, when he has only a set of handicraftsmen to feed, and I my liberally-educated household.

Soc. What is a handicraftsman? Does not the term apply to all who can make any sort of useful product or commodity?

Ar. Certainly.

Soc. Barley meal is a useful product, is it not?

Ar. Pre-eminently so.

Soc. And loaves of bread?

Ar. No less.

Soc. Well, and what do you say to cloaks for men and for women - tunics, mantles, vests?[4]

[4] For these articles of dress see Becker's "Charicles," Exc. i. to Sc. xi. "Dress."

Ar. Yes, they are all highly useful commodities.

Soc. Then your household do not know how to make any of these?

Ar. On the contrary, I believe they can make them all.

Soc. Then you are not aware that by means of the manufacture of one of these alone - his barley meal store - Nausicydes[5] not only maintains himself and his domestics, but many pigs and cattle besides, and realises such large profits that he frequently contributes to the state benevolences;[6] while there is Cyrebus, again, who, out of a bread factory, more than maintains the whole of his establishment, and lives in the lap of luxury; and Demeas of Collytus gets a livelihood out of a cloak business, and Menon as a mantua-maker, and so, again, more than half the Megarians[7] by the making of vests.

[5] Nausicydes. Cobet, "Pros. Xen." cf. Aristoph. "Eccles." 426.

[6] Lit. "state liturgies," or "to the burden of the public services." For these see Gow, "Companion," xviii. "Athenian Finance."

[7] Cf. Arist. "Acharnians," 519, {esukophantei Megareon ta khlaniskia}. See Dr. Merry's note ad loc.

Ar. Bless me, yes! They have got a set of barbarian fellows, whom they purchase and keep, to manufacture by forced labour whatever takes their fancy. My kinswomen, I need not tell you, are free-born ladies.

Soc. Then, on the ground that they are free-born and your kinswomen, you think that they ought to do nothing but eat and sleep? Or is it your opinion that people who live in this way - I speak of free-born people in general - lead happier lives, and are more to be congratulated, than those who give their time and attention to such useful arts of life as they are skilled in? Is this what you see in the world, that for the purpose of learning what it is well to know, and of recollecting the lessons taught, or with a view to health and strength of body, or for the sake of acquiring and preserving all that gives life its charm, idleness and inattention are found to be helpful, whilst work and study are simply a dead loss? Pray, when those relatives of yours were taught what you tell me they know, did they learn it as barren information which they would never turn to practical account, or, on the contrary, as something with which they were to be seriously concerned some day, and from which they were to reap advantage? Do human beings in general attain to well-tempered manhood by a course of idling, or by carefully attending to what will be of use? Which will help a man the more to grow in justice and uprightness, to be up and doing, or to sit with folded hands revolving the ways and means of existence? As things now stand, if I am not mistaken, there is no love lost between you. You cannot help feeling that they are costly to you, and they must see that you find them a burthen? This is a perilous state of affairs, in which hatred and bitterness have every prospect of increasing, whilst the pre-existing bond of affection[8] is likely to be snapped.

[8] Or, "the original stock of kindliness will be used up."

But now, if only you allow them free scope for their energies, when you come to see how useful they can be, you will grow quite fond of them, and they, when they perceive that they can please you, will cling to their benefactor warmly. Thus, with the memory of former kindnesses made sweeter, you will increase the grace which flows from kindnesses tenfold; you will in consequence be knit in closer bonds of love and domesticity. If, indeed, they were called upon to do any shameful work, let them choose death rather than that; but now they know, it would seem, the very arts and accomplishments which are regarded as the loveliest and the most suitable for women; and the things which we know, any of us, are just those which we can best perform, that is to say, with ease and expedition; it is a joy to do them, and the result is beautiful.[9] Do not hesitate, then, to initiate your friends in what will bring advantage to them and you alike; probably they will gladly respond to your summons.

[9] Or, "with ease, rapidity, pleasure and effect."

Well, upon my word (Aristarchus answered), I like so well what you say, Socrates, that though hitherto I have not been disposed to borrow, knowing that when I had spent what I got I should not be in a condition to repay, I think I can now bring myself to do so in order to raise a fund for these works.

Thereupon a capital was provided; wools were purchased; the good man's relatives set to work, and even whilst they breakfasted they worked, and on and on till work was ended and they supped. Smiles took the place of frowns; they no longer looked askance with suspicion, but full into each other's eyes with happiness. They loved their kinsman for his kindness to them. He became attached to them as helpmates; and the end of it all was, he came to Socrates and told him with delight how matters fared; "and now," he added, "they tax me with being the only drone in the house, who sit and eat the bread of idleness."

To which Socrates: Why do not you tell them the fable of the dog?[10] Once on a time, so goes the story, when beasts could speak, the sheep said to her master, "What a marvel is this, master, that to us, your own sheep, who provide you with fleeces and lambs and cheese, you give nothing, save only what we may nibble off earth's bosom; but with this dog of yours, who provides you with nothing of the sort, you share the very meat out of your mouth." When the dog heard these words, he answered promptly, "Ay, in good sooth, for is it not I who keep you safe and sound, you sheep, so that you are not stolen by man nor harried by wolves; since, if I did not keep watch over you, you would not be able so much as to graze afield, fearing to be destroyed." And so, says the tale, the sheep had to admit that the dog was rightly preferred to themselves in honour. And so do you tell your flock yonder that like the dog in the fable you are their guardian and overseer, and it is thanks to you that they are protected from evil and evildoers, so that they work their work and live their lives in blissful security.

[10] See Joseph Jacobs, "The Fables of Aesop," vol. i. p. 26 foll., for "a complete list of the Fables given in Greek literature up to the fall of Greek independence." Cf. Hesiod, "Works and Days," 202 foll.; Archilochus, 89 (60), Bergk; Herod. i. 141; Aesch. "Myrmid." fr. 123; Aristot. "Rhet." II. xx.

VIII

At another time chancing upon an old friend whom he had not seen for a long while, he greeted him thus.

Soc. What quarter of the world do you hail from, Eutherus?

The other answered: From abroad, just before the close of the war; but at present from the city itself. [1] You see, since we have been denuded of our possessions across the frontier,[2] and my father left me nothing in Attica, I must needs bide at home, and provide myself with the necessaries of life by means of bodily toil, which seems preferable to begging from another, especially as I have no security on which to raise a loan.

[1] Lit. "from here." The conversation perhaps takes place in Piraeus 404 B.C.
[2] Or, "colonial possession." Cf. "Symp." iv. 31.

Soc. And how long do you expect your body to be equal to providing the necessaries of life for hire?
Euth. Goodness knows, Socrates - not for long.
Soc. And when you find yourself an old man, expenses will not diminish, and yet no one will care to pay you for the labour of your hands.
Euth. That is true.
Soc. Would it not be better then to apply yourself at once to such work as will stand you in good stead when you are old - that is, address yourself to some large proprietor who needs an assistant in managing his estate?[3] By superintending his works, helping to get in his crops, and guarding his property in general, you will be a benefit to the estate and be benefited in return.

[3] Cf. "Cyrop." VIII. Iii. 48.

I could not endure the yoke of slavery, Socrates! (he exclaimed).
Soc. And yet the heads of departments in a state are not regarded as adopting the badge of slavery because they manage the public property, but as having attained a higher degree of freedom rather.
Euth. In a word, Socrates, the idea of being held to account to another is not at all to my taste.
Soc. And yet, Eutherus, it would be hard to find a work which did not involve some liability to account; in fact it is difficult to do anything without some mistake or other, and no less difficult, if you should succeed in doing it immaculately, to escape all unfriendly criticism. I wonder now whether you find it easy to get through your present occupations entirely without reproach. No? Let me tell you what you should do. You should avoid censorious persons and attach yourself to the considerate and kind-hearted, and in all your affairs accept with a good grace what you can and decline what you feel you cannot do. Whatever it be, do it heart and soul, and make it your finest work.[4] There lies the method at once to silence fault-finders and to minister help to your own difficulties. Life will flow smoothly, risks will be diminished, provision against old age secured.

[4] Or, "study to make it your finest work, the expression of a real enthusiasm."

IX

At another time, as I am aware, he had heard a remark made by Crito[1] that life at Athens was no easy matter for a man who wished to mind his own affairs.

[1] Crito. See above, I. ii. 48; Cobet, "P. X."; cf. Plat. "Rep." viii. 549 C.

As, for instance, at this moment (Crito proceeded) there are a set of fellows threatening me with lawsuits, not because they have any misdemeanour to allege against me, but simply under the conviction that I will sooner pay a sum of money than be troubled further.
To which Socrates replied: Tell me, Crito, you keep dogs, do you not, to ward off wolves from your flocks?

Cr. Certainly; it pays to do so.

Soc. Then why do you not keep a watchman willing and competent to ward off this pack of people who seek to injure you?

I should not at all mind (he answered), if I were not afraid he might turn again and rend his keeper.

What! (rejoined Socrates), do you not see that to gratify a man like yourself is far pleasanter as a matter of self-interest than to quarrel with you? You may be sure there are plenty of people here who will take the greatest pride in making you their friend.

Accordingly, they sought out Archedemus,[2] a practical man with a clever tongue in his head[3] but poor; the fact being, he was not the sort to make gain by hook or by crook, but a lover of honesty and of too good a nature himself to make his living as a pettifogger.[4] Crito would then take the opportunity of times of harvesting and put aside small presents for Achedemus of corn and oil, or wine, or wool, or any other of the farm produce forming the staple commodities of life, or he would invite him to a sacrificial feast, and otherwise pay him marked attention. Archedemus, feeling that he had in Crito's house a harbour of refuge, could not make too much of his patron, and ere long he had hunted up a long list of iniquities which could be lodged against Crito's pettifogging persecutors themselves, and not only their numerous crimes but their numerous enemies; and presently he prosecuted one of them in a public suit, where sentence would be given against him "what to suffer or what to pay."[5] The accused, conscious as he was of many rascally deeds, did all he could to be quit of Archedemus, but Archedemus was not to be got rid of. He held on until he had made the informer not only loose his hold of Crito but pay himself a sum of money; and now that Archedemus had achieved this and other similar victories, it is easy to guess what followed.[6] It was just as when some shepherd has got a very good dog, all the other shepherds wish to lodge their flocks in his neighbourhood that they too may reap the benefit of him. So a number of Crito's friends came begging him to allow Archedemus to be their guardian also, and Archedemus was overjoyed to do something to gratify Crito, and so it came about that not only Crito abode in peace, but his friends likewise. If any of those people with whom Archedemus was not on the best of terms were disposed to throw it in his teeth that he accepted his patron's benefits and paid in flatteries, he had a ready retort: "Answer me this question - which is the more scandalous, to accept kindnesses from honest folk and to repay them, with the result that I make such people my friends but quarrel with knaves, or to make enemies of honourable gentlemen[7] by attempts to do them wrong, with the off-chance indeed of winning the friendship of some scamps in return for my co-operation, but the certainty of losing in the tone of my acquaintances?"[8]

[2] Archedemus, possibly the demagogue, "Hell." I. vii. 2. So Cobet, "P. X.," but see Grote, "H. G." viii. 245.

[3] Lit. "very capable of speech and action" - the writer's favourite formula for the well-trained Athenian who can speak fluently and reason clearly, and act energetically and opportunely.

[4] Reading {kai euphuesteros on} [or {e os}] . . . {apo sukophanton} [or {sukophantion}], after Cobet, "P. X." s.v. Archedemus. The MSS. give {kai ephe raston einai} - "nothing is easier," he said, "than recovering from sycophants."

[5] For this formula cf. "Econ." vi. 24. Cf. Plat. "Statesm." 299 A.

[6] {ede tote}. Cf. Plat. "Laws," vi. 778 C.

[7] Lit. the {kaloi kagathoi}, which like {khrestous} and {ponerous} has a political as well as an ethical meaning.

[8] Lit. "must associate with these (the {ponerois}) instead of those (the {kalois te kagathois})."

The net result of the whole proceedings was that Archedemus was now Crito's right hand,[9] and by the rest of Crito's friends he was held in honour.

[9] He was No. 1 - {eis}.

X

Again I may cite, as known to myself,[1] the following discussion; the arguments were addressed to Diodorus, one of his companions. The master said:

[1] Or, "for which I can personally vouch."

Tell me, Diodorus, if one of your slaves runs away, are you at pains to recover him?

More than that (Diodorus answered), I summon others to my aid and I have a reward cried for his recovery.

Soc. Well, if one of your domestics is sick, do you tend him and call in the doctors to save his life?

Diod. Decidedly I do.

Soc. And if an intimate acquaintance who is far more precious to you than any of your household slaves is about to perish of want, you would think it incumbent on you to take pains to save his life? Well! now you know without my telling you that Hermogenes[2] is not made of wood or stone. If you helped him he would be ashamed not to pay you in kind. And yet - the opportunity of possessing a willing, kindly, and trusty assistant well fitted to do your bidding, and not merely that, but capable of originating useful ideas himself, with a certain forecast of mind and judgment - I say such a man is worth dozens of slaves. Good economists tell us that when a precious article may be got at a low price we ought to buy. And nowadays when times are so bad it is possible to get good friends exceedingly cheap.

[2] Hermogenes, presumably the son of Hipponicus. See I. ii. 48.

Diodorus answered: You are quite right, Socrates; bid Hermogenes come to me.

Soc. Bid Hermogenes come to you! - not I indeed! since for aught I can understand you are no better entitled to summon him that to go to him yourself, nor is the advantage more on his side than your own.

Thus Diodorus went off in a trice to seek Hermogenes, and at no great outlay won to himself a friend - a friend whose one concern it now was to discover how, by word or deed, he might help and gladden Diodorus.

BOOK III

I

Aspirants to honour and distinction[1] derived similar help from Socrates, who in each case stimulated in them a persevering assiduity towards their several aims, as the following narratives tend to show. He had heard on one occasion of the arrival in Athens of Dionysodorus,[2] who professed to teach the whole duty of a general.[3] Accordingly he remarked to one of those who were with him - a young man whose anxiety to obtain the office of Strategos[4] was no secret to him:

[1] *{ton kalon}* = *everything which the {kalos te kagathos} should aim at, but especially the honourable offices of state such as the Archonship, Strategia, Hipparchia, etc. See Plat. "Laches."*
[2] *Dionysodorus of Chios, presumably. See Plat. "Euthyd." 271 C foll.*
[3] *A professor of the science and art of strategy.*
[4] *Lit. "that honour," sc. the Strategia.*

Soc. It would be monstrous on the part of any one who sought to become a general[5] to throw away the slightest opportunity of learning the duties of the office. Such a person, I should say, would deserve to be fined and punished by the state far more than the charlatan who without having learnt the art of a sculptor undertakes a contract to carve a statue. Considering that the whole fortunes of the state are entrusted to the general during a war, with all its incidental peril, it is only reasonable to anticipate that great blessings or great misfortunes will result in proportion to the success or bungling of that officer. I appeal to you, young sir, do you not agree that a candidate who, while taking pains to be elected neglects to learn the duties of the office, would richly deserve to be fined?

[5] *i.e. "head of the war department, and commander-in-chief," etc.*

With arguments like these he persuaded the young man to go and take lessons. After he had gone through the course he came back, and Socrates proceeded playfully to banter him.

Soc. Behold our young friend, sirs, as Homer says of Agamemnon, of mein majestical,[6] so he; does he not seem to move more majestically, like one who has studied to be a general? Of course, just as a man who has learned to play the harp is a harper, even if he never touch the instrument, or as one who has studied medicine is a physician, though he does not practise, so our friend here from this time forward is now and ever shall be a general, even though he does not receive a vote at the elections. But the dunce who has not the science is neither general nor doctor, no, not even if the whole world appointed him. But (he proceeded, turning to the youth), in case any of us should ever find ourselves captain or colonel[7] under you, to give us some smattering of the science of war, what did the professor take as the starting-point of his instruction in generalship? Please inform us.

[6] *"Il." iii. 169, 170.*
[7] *Or, "brigadier or captain," lit. taxiarch or lochagos.*

Then the young man: He began where he ended; he taught me tactics[8] - tactics and nothing else.

[8] *Cf. "Cyrop." I. vi. 12 foll.; VIII. v. 15.*

Yet surely (replied Socrates) that is only an infinitisemal part of generalship. A general[9] must be ready in furnishing the material of war: in providing the commissariat for his troops; quick in devices, he must be full of practical resource; nothing must escape his eye or tax his endurance; he must be shrewd, and ready of wit, a combination at once of clemency and fierceness, of simplicity and of insidious craft; he must play the part of watchman, of robber; now prodigal as a spendthrift, and again close-fisted as a miser, the bounty of his munificence must be equalled by the narrowness of his greed; impregnable in defence, a very dare-devil in attack - these and many other qualities must he possess who is to make a good general and minister of war; they must come to him by gift of nature or through science. No doubt it is a grand thing also to be a tactician, since there is all the difference in the world between an army properly handled in the field and the same in disorder; just as stones and bricks, woodwork and tiles, tumbled together in a heap are of no use at all, but arrange them in a certain order - at bottom and atop materials which will not crumble or rot, such as stones and earthen tiles, and in the middle between the two put bricks and woodwork, with an eye to architectural principle,[10] and finally you get a valuable possession - to wit, a dwelling-place.

[9] A strategos. For the duties and spheres of action of this officer, see Gow, op. cit. xiv. 58.
[10] "As in the building of a house." See Vitrivius, ii. 3; Plin. Xxv. 14.

The simile is very apt, Socrates[11] (replied the youth), for in battle, too, the rule is to draw up the best men in front and rear, with those of inferior quality between, where they may be led on by the former and pushed on by the hinder.

[11] Cf. "Il." iv. 297 foll.; "Cyrop." VI. iii. 25; Polyb. x. 22.

Soc. Very good, no doubt, if the professor taught you to distinguish good and bad; but if not, where is the use of your learning? It would scarcely help you, would it, to be told to arrange coins in piles, the best coins at top and bottom and the worst in the middle, unless you were first taught to distinguish real from counterfeit.

The Youth. Well no, upon my word, he did not teach us that, so that the task of distinguishing between good and bad must devolve on ourselves.

Soc. Well, shall we see, then, how we may best avoid making blunders between them?

I am ready (replied the youth).

Soc. Well then! Let us suppose we are marauders, and the task imposed upon us is to carry off some bullion; it will be a right disposition of our forces if we place in the vanguard those who are the greediest of gain?[12]

[12] "Whose fingers itch for gold."

The Youth. I should think so.

Soc. Then what if there is danger to be faced? Shall the vanguard consist of men who are greediest of honour?

The Youth. It is these, at any rate, who will face danger for the sake of praise and glory.[13] Fortunately such people are not hid away in a corner; they shine forth conspicuous everywhere, and are easy to be discovered.

[13] Cf. Shakesp. "seeking the bubble reputation even in the cannon's mouth."

Soc. But tell me, did he teach you how to draw up troops in general, or specifically where and how to apply each particular kind of tactical arrangement?

The Youth. Nothing of the sort.

Soc. And yet there are and must be innumerable circumstances in which the same ordering of march or battle will be out of place.

The Youth. I assure you he did not draw any of these fine distinctions.

He did not, did not he? (he answered). Bless me! Go back to him again, then, and ply him with questions; if he really has the science, and is not lost to all sense of shame, he will blush to have taken your money and then to have sent you away empty.

II

At another time he fell in with a man who had been chosen general and minister of war, and thus accosted him.

Soc. Why did Homer, think you, designate Agamemnon "shepherd of the peoples"?[1] Was it possibly to show that, even as a shepherd must care for his sheep and see that they are safe and have all things needful, and that the objects of their rearing be secured, so also must a general take care that his soldiers are safe and have their supplies, and attain the objects of their soldiering? Which last is that they may get the mastery of their enemies, and so add to their own good fortune and happiness; or tell me, what made him praise Agamemnon, saying -

He is both a good king and a warrior bold?[2]

Did he mean, perhaps, to imply that he would be a 'warrior bold,' not merely in standing alone and bravely battling against the foe, but as inspiring the whole of his host with like prowess; and by a 'good king,' not merely one who should stand forth gallantly to protect his own life, but who should be the source of happiness to all over whom he reigns? Since a man is not chosen king in order to take heed to himself, albeit nobly, but that those who chose him may attain to happiness through him. And why do men go soldiering except to ameliorate existence?[3] and to this end they choose their generals that they may find in them guides to the goal in question. He, then, who undertakes that office is bound to procure for those who choose him the thing they seek for. And indeed it were not easy to find any nobler ambition than this, or aught ignobler than its opposite.

[1] "Il." ii. 243. "The People's Paster," Chapman.
[2] "Il." iii. 179; cf. "Symp." iv. 6. A favourite line of Alexander the Great's, it is said.
[3] Of, "that life may reach some flower of happiness."

After such sort he handled the question, what is the virtue of a good leader? and by shredding off all superficial qualities, laid bare as the kernel of the matter that it is the function of every leader to make those happy whom he may be called upon to lead.[4]

[4] Cf. Plat. "Rep." 342.

III

The following conversation with a youth who had just been elected hipparch[1] (or commandant of cavalry), I can also vouch for.[2]

[1] Cf. "Hipparch."
[2] Lit. "I know he once held."

Soc. Can you tell us what set you wishing to be a general of cavalry, young sir? What was your object? I suppose it was not simply to ride at the head of the "knights," an honour not denied to the mounted archers,[3] who ride even in front of the generals themselves?

[3] Lit. "Hippotoxotai." See Boeckh, "P. E. A." II. xxi. p. 264 (Eng. tr.)

Hipp. You are right.

Soc. No more was it for the sake merely of public notoriety, since a madman might boast of that fatal distinction.[4]

[4] Or, "as we all know, 'Tom Fool' can boast," etc.

Hipp. You are right again.

Soc. Is this possibly the explanation? you think to improve the cavalry - your aim would be to hand it over to the state in better condition than you find it; and, if the cavalry chanced to be called out, you at their head would be the cause of some good thing to Athens?

Hipp. Most certainly.

Soc. Well, and a noble ambition too, upon my word - if you can achieve your object. The command to which you are appointed concerns horses and riders, does it not?

Hipp. It does, no doubt.

Soc. Come then, will you explain to us first how you propose to improve the horses.

Hipp. Ah, that will scarcely form part of my business, I fancy. Each trooper is personally responsible for the condition of his horse.

Soc. But suppose, when they present themselves and their horses,[5] you find that some have brought beasts with bad feet or legs or otherwise infirm, and others such ill-fed jades that they cannot keep up on the march; others, again, brutes so ill broken and unmanageable that they will not keep their place in the ranks, and others such desperate plungers that they cannot be got to any place in the ranks at all. What becomes of your cavalry force then? How will you charge at the head of such a troop, and win glory for the state?

[5] For this phrase, see Schneider and Kuhner ad loc.

Hipp. You are right. I will try to look after the horses to my utmost.

Soc. Well, and will you not lay your hand to improve the men themselves?

Hipp. I will.

Soc. The first thing will be to make them expert in mounting their chargers?

Hipp. That certainly, for if any of them were dismounted he would then have a better chance of saving himself.

Soc. Well, but when it comes to the hazard of engagement, what will you do then? Give orders to draw the enemy down to the sandy ground[6] where you are accustomed to manouvre, or endeavour beforehand to put your men through their practice on ground resembling a real battlefield?

[6] e.g. the hippodrome at Phaleron.

Hipp. That would be better, no doubt.

Soc. Well, shall you regard it as a part of your duty to see that as many of your men as possible can take aim and shoot on horseback?[7]

[7] Cf. "Hipparch," i. 21.

Hipp. It will be better, certainly.

Soc. And have you thought how to whet the courage of your troopers? to kindle in them rage to meet the enemy? - which things are but stimulants to make stout hearts stouter?

Hipp. If I have not done so hitherto, I will try to make up for lost time now.

Soc. And have you troubled your head at all to consider how you are to secure the obedience of your men? for without that not one particle of good will you get, for all your horses and troopers so brave and so stout.

Hipp. That is a true saying; but how, Socrates, should a man best bring them to this virtue?[8]

Soc. I presume you know that in any business whatever, people are more apt to follow the lead of those whom they look upon as adepts; thus in case of sickness they are readiest to obey him whom they regard as the cleverest physician; and so on a voyage the most skilful pilot; in matters agricultural the best farmer, and so forth.

Hipp. Yes, certainly.

Soc. Then in this matter of cavalry also we may reasonably suppose that he who is looked upon as knowing his business best will command the readiest obedience.

Hipp. If, then, I can prove to my troopers that I am better than all of them, will that suffice to win their obedience?

Soc. Yes, if along with that you can teach them that obedience to you brings greater glory and surer safety to themselves.

Hipp. How am I to teach them that?

Soc. Upon my word! How are you to teach them that? Far more easily, I take it, than if you had to teach them that bad things are better than good, and more advantageous to boot.

Hipp. I suppose you mean that, besides his other qualifications a commandant of cavalry must have command of speech and argument?[9]

[9] Or, "practise the art of oratory"; "express himself clearly and rationally." See Grote, "H. G." VIII. lxvii. p. 463 note; "Hipparch," i. 24; viii. 22.

Soc. Were you under the impression that the commandant was not to open his mouth? Did it never occur to you that all the noblest things which custom[10] compels us to learn, and to which indeed we owe our knowledge of life, have all been learned by means of speech[11] and reason; and if there be any other noble learning which a man may learn, it is this same reason whereby he learns it; and the best teachers are those who have the freest command of thought and language, and those that have the best knowledge of the most serious things are the most brilliant masters of disputation. Again, have you not observed that whenever this city of ours fits out one of her choruses - such as that, for instance, which is sent to Delos[12] - there is nothing elsewhere from any quarter of the world which can compete with it; nor will you find in any other state collected so fair a flower of manhood as in Athens?[13]

[10] Cf Arist. "Rhet." ii. 12, {oi neoi pepaideuntai upo tou nomou monon}.
[11] {dia logou}.
[12] See Thuc. iii. 104; and below, IV. viii. 2.
[13] See references ap. Schneider and Kuhner; "Symp." iv. 17.

Hipp. You say truly.

Soc. But for all that, it is not in sweetness of voice that the Athenians differ from the rest of the world so much, nor in stature of body or strength of limb, but in ambition and that love of honour[14] which most of all gives a keen edge to the spirit in the pursuit of things lovely and of high esteem.

[14] See below, v. 3; Dem. "de Cor." 28 foll.

Hipp. That, too, is a true saying.

Soc. Do you not think, then, that if a man devoted himself to our cavalry also, here in Athens, we should far outstrip the rest of the world, whether in the furnishing of arms and horses, or in orderliness of battle-array, or in eager hazardous encounter with the foe, if only we could persuade ourselves that by so doing we should obtain honour and distinction?

Hipp. It is reasonable to think so.

Soc. Have no hesitation, therefore, but try to guide your men into this path,[15] whence you yourself, and through you your fellow- citizens, will reap advantage.

[15] Or, "to conduct which will not certainly fail of profit to yourself or through you to . . ."

Yes, in good sooth, I will try (he answered).

IV

At another time, seeing Nicomachides on his way back from the elections (of magistrates),[1] he asked him: Who are elected generals, Nicomachides?

[1] Cf. "Pol. Ath." i. 3; Aristot. "Ath. Pol." 44. 4; and Dr. Sandys' note ad loc. p. 165 of his edition.

And he: Is it not just like them, these citizens of Athens - just like them, I say - to go and elect, not me, who ever since my name first apepared on the muster-roll have literally worn myself out with military service - now as a captain, now as a colonel - and have received all these wounds from the enemy, look you! (at the same time, and suiting the action to the word, he bared his arms and proceeded to show the scars of ancient wounds) - they elect not me (he went on), but, if you please, Antisthenes! who never served as a hoplite[2] in his life nor in the cavalry ever made a brilliant stroke, that I ever heard tell of; no! in fact, he has got no science at all, I take it, except to amass stores of wealth.

[2] Cf. Lys. Xiv. 10.

But still (returned Socrates), surely that is one point in his favour - he ought to be able to provide the troops with supplies.

Nic. Well, for the matter of that, merchants are good hands at collecting stores; but it does not follow that a merchant or trader will be able to command an army.

But (rejoined Socrates) Antisthenes is a man of great pertinacity, who insists on winning, and that is a very necessary quality in a general.[3] Do not you see how each time he has been choragos[4] he has been successful with one chorus after another?

[3] See Grote, "Plato," i. 465 foll.
[4] Choir-master, or Director of the Chorus. It was his duty to provide and preside over a chorus to sing, dance, or play at any of the public festivals, defraying the cost as a state service of {leitourgia}. See "Pol. Ath." iii. 4; "Hiero," ix. 4; Aristot. "Pol. Ath." 28. 3.

Nic. Bless me! yes; but there is a wide difference between standing at the head of a band of singers and dancers and a troop of soldiers.

Soc. Still, without any practical skill in singing or in the training of a chorus, Antisthenes somehow had the art to select the greatest proficients in both.

Nic. Yes, and by the same reasoning we are to infer that on a campaign he will find proficients, some to marshal the troops for him and others to fight his battles?

Soc. Just so. If in matters military he only exhibits the same skill in selecting the best hands as he has shown in matters of the chorus, it is highly probable he will here also bear away the palm of victory; and we may presume that if he expended so much to win a choric victory with a single tribe,[5] he will be ready to expend more to secure a victory in war with the whole state to back him.

[5] See Dem. "against Lept." 496. 26. Each tribe nominated such of its members as were qualified to undertake the burden.

Nic. Do you really mean, Socrates, that it is the function of the same man to provide efficient choruses and to act as commander-in-chief?
Soc. I mean this, that, given a man knows what he needs to provide, and has the skill to do so, no matter what the deparment of things may be - house or city or army - you will find him a good chief and director[6] of the same.

[6] Or, "representative."

Then Nicomachides: Upon my word, Socrates, I should never have expected to hear you say that a good housekeeper[7] and steward of an estate would make a good general.

[7] Or, "economist"; cf. "Cyrop." I. vi. 12.

Soc. Come then, suppose we examine their respective duties, and so determine[8] whether they are the same or different.

[8] Lit. "get to know."

Nic. Let us do so.
Soc. Well then, is it not a common duty of both to procure the ready obedience of those under them to their orders?
Nic. Certainly.
Soc. And also to assign to those best qualified to perform them their distinctive tasks?
That, too, belongs to both alike (he answered).
Soc. Again, to chastise the bad and reward the good belongs to both alike, methinks?
Nic. Decidedly.
Soc. And to win the kindly feeling of their subordinates must surely be the noble ambition of both?
That too (he answered).
Soc. And do you consider it to the interest of both alike to win the adherence of supporters and allies?
[9]

[9] In reference to the necessity of building up a family connection or political alliances cf. Arist. "Pol." iii. 9, 13.

Nic. Without a doubt.
Soc. And does it not closely concern them both to be good guardians of their respective charges?
Nic. Very much so.
Soc. Then it equally concerns them both to be painstaking and prodigal of toil in all their doings?
Nic. Yes, all these duties belong to both alike, but the parallel ends when you come to actual fighting.
Soc. Yet they are both sure to meet with enemies?
Nic. There is no doubt about that.
Soc. Then is it not to the interest of both to get the upper hand of these?

Nic. Certainly; but you omit to tell us what service organisation and the art of management will render when it comes to actual fighting.

Soc. Why, it is just then, I presume, it will be of most service, for the good economist knows that nothing is so advantageous or so lucrative as victory in battle, or to put it negatively, nothing so disastrous and expensive as defeat. He will enthusiastically seek out and provide everything conducive to victory, he will painstakingly discover and guard against all that tends to defeat, and when satisifed that all is ready and ripe for victory he will deliver battle energetically, and what is equally important, until the hour of final preparation has arrived,[10] he will be cautious to deliver battle. Do not despise men of economic genius, Nicomachides; the difference between the devotion requisite to private affairs and to affairs of state is merely one of quantity. For the rest the parallel holds strictly, and in this respect pre-eminently, that both are concerned with human instruments: which human beings, moreover, are of one type and temperament, whether we speak of devotion to public affairs or of the administration of private property. To fare well in either case is given to those who know the secret of dealing with humanity, whereas the absence of that knowledge will as certainly imply in either case a fatal note of discord.[11]

[10] Lit. "as long as he is unprepared."

[11] L. Dindorf, "Index Graec." Ox. ed.; cf. Hor. "Ep." II. ii. 144, "sed verae numerosque modosque ediscere vitae," "the harmony of life," Conington.

V

A conversation held with Pericles the son of the great statesman may here be introduced.[1] Socrates began:

[1] Or, "On one occasion Pericles was the person addressed in conversation." For Pericles see "Hell." I. v. 16; vii. 15; Plut. "Pericl." 37 (Clough, i. 368).

I am looking forward, I must tell you, Pericles, to a great improvement in our military affairs when you are minister of war.[2] The prestige of Athens, I hope, will rise; we shall gain the mastery over our enemies.

[2] "Strategos."

Pericles replied: I devoutly wish your words might be fulfilled, but how this happy result is to be obtained, I am at a loss to discover.

Shall we (Socrates continued), shall we balance the arguments for and against, and consider to what extent the possibility does exist?

Pray let us do so (he answered).

Soc. Well then, you know that in point of numbers the Athenians are not inferior to the Boeotians?

Per. Yes, I am aware of that.

Soc. And do you think the Boeotians could furnish a better pick of fine healthy men than the Athenians?

Per. I think we should very well hold our own in that respect.

Soc. And which of the two would you take to be the more united people - the friendlier among themselves?

Per. The Athenians, I should say, for so many sections of the Boeotians, resenting the selfish policy[3] of Thebes, are ill disposed to that power, but at Athens I see nothing of the sort.

[3] "The self-aggrandisement."

Soc. But perhaps you will say that there is no people more jealous of honour or haughtier in spirit.[4] And these feelings are no weak spurs to quicken even a dull spirit to hazard all for glory's sake and fatherland.

[4] Reading {megalophronestatoi}, after Cobet. See "Hipparch," vii. 3; or if as vulg. {philophronestatoi}, transl. "more affable."

Per. Nor is there much fault to find with Athenians in these respects.
Soc. And if we turn to consider the fair deeds of ancestry,[5] to no people besides ourselves belongs so rich a heritage of stimulating memories, whereby so many of us are stirred to pursue virtue with devotion and to show ourselves in our turn also men of valour like our sires.

[5] See Wesley's anthem, Eccles. xliv. 1, "Let us now praise famous men and our fathers that begat us."

Per. All that you say, Socrates, is most true, but do you observe that ever since the disaster of the thousand under Tolmides at Lebadeia, coupled with that under Hippocrates at Delium,[6] the prestige of Athens by comparison with the Boeotians has been lowered, whilst the spirit of Thebes as against Athens had been correspondingly exalted, so that those Boeotians who in old days did not venture to give battle to the Athenians even in their own territory unless they had the Lacedaemonians and the rest of the Peloponnesians to help them, do nowadays threaten to make an incursion into Attica single-handed; and the Athenians, who formerly, if they had to deal with the Boeotians[7] only, made havoc of their territory, are now afraid the Boeotians may some day harry Attica.

[6] Lebadeia, 447 B.C.; Delium, 424 B.C. For Tolmides and Hippocrates see Thuc. i. 113; iv. 100 foll.; Grote, "H. G." v. 471; vi. 533.
[7] Reading {ote B. monoi}, al. {ou monoi}, "when the Boeotians were not unaided."

To which Socrates: Yes, I perceive that this is so, but it seems to me that the state was never more tractably disposed, never so ripe for a really good leader, as to-day. For if boldness be the parent of carelessness, laxity, and insubordination, it is the part of fear to make people more disposed to application, obedience, and good order. A proof of which you may discover in the behaviour of people on ship- board. It is in seasons of calm weather when there is nothing to fear that disorder may be said to reign, but as soon as there is apprehension of a storm, or an enemy in sight, the scene changes; not only is each word of command obeyed, but there is a hush of silent expectation; the mariners wait to catch the next signal like an orchestra with eyes upon the leader.
Per. But indeed, given that now is the opportunity to take obedience at the flood, it is high time also to explain by what means we are to rekindle in the hearts of our countrymen[8] the old fires - the passionate longing for antique valour, for the glory and the wellbeing of the days of old.

[8] Reading {anerasthenai}, Schneider's emendation of the vulg. {aneristhenai}.

Well (proceeded Socrates), supposing we wished them to lay claim to certain material wealth now held by others, we could not better stimulate them to lay hands on the objects coveted than by showing them that these were ancestral possessions[9] to which they had a natural right. But since our object is that they should set their hearts on virtuous pre-eminence, we must prove to them that such headship combined with virtue is an old time-honoured heritage which pertains to them beyond all others, and that if they strive earnestly after it they will soon out-top the world.

[9] Cf. Solon in the matter of Salamis, Plut. "Sol." 8; Bergk. "Poet. Lyr. Gr. Solon," SALAMIS, i. 2, 3.

Por. How are we to inculcate this lesson?

Soc. I think by reminding them of a fact already registered in their minds,[10] that the oldest of our ancestors whose names are known to us were also the bravest of heroes.

[10] Or, "to which their ears are already opened."

Per. I suppose you refer to that judgment of the gods which, for their virtue's sake, Cecrops and his followers were called on to decide?[11]

[11] See Apollodorus, iii. 14.

Soc. Yes, I refer to that and to the birth and rearing of Erectheus,[12] and also to the war[13] which in his days was waged to stay the tide of invasion from the whole adjoining continent; and that other war in the days of the Heraclidae[14] against the men of Peloponnese; and that series of battles fought in the days of Theseus[15] - in all which the virtuous pre-eminence of our ancestry above the men of their own times was made manifest. Or, if you please, we may come down to things of a later date, which their descendants and the heroes of days not so long anterior to our own wrought in the struggle with the lords of Asia,[16] nay of Europe also, as far as Macedonia: a people possessing a power and means of attack far exceeding any who had gone before - who, moreover, had accomplished the doughtiest deeds. These things the men of Athens wrought partly single-handed,[17] and partly as sharers with the Peloponnesians in laurels won by land and sea. Heroes were these men also, far outshining, as tradition tells us, the peoples of their time.

[12] Cf. "Il." ii. 547, {'Erekhtheos megaletoros k.t.l.}
[13] Cf. Isoc. "Paneg." 19, who handles all the topics.
[14] Commonly spoken of as "the Return." See Grote, "H. G." II. ch. xviii.
[15] Against the Amazons and Thracians; cf. Herod. ix. 27; Plut. "Thes." 27.
[16] The "Persian" wars; cf. Thucyd. I. i.
[17] He omits the Plataeans.

Per. Yes, so runs the story of their heroism.

Soc. Therefore it is that, amidst the many changes of inhabitants, and the migrations which have, wave after wave, swept over Hellas, these maintained themselves in their own land, unmoved; so that it was a common thing for others to turn to them as to a court of appeal on points of right, or to flee to Athens as a harbour of refuge from the hand of the oppressor.[18]

[18] Cf. (Plat.) "Menex."; Isocr. "Paneg."

Then Pericles: And the wonder to me, Socrates, is how our city ever came to decline.

Soc. I think we are victims of our own success. Like some athlete,[19] whose facile preponderance in the arena has betrayed him into laxity until he eventually succumbs to punier antagonists, so we Athenians, in the plenitude of our superiority, have neglected ourselves and are become degenerate.

[19] Reading {athletai tines}, or if {alloi tines}, translate "any one else."

Per. What then ought we to do now to recover our former virtue?

Soc. There need be no mystery about that, I think. We can rediscover the institutions of our forefathers - applying them to the regulation of our lives with something of their precision, and not improbably with like success; or we can imitate those who stand at the front of affairs to-day,[20] adapting to ourselves their rule of life, in which case, if we live up to the standard of our models, we may hope at least to rival their excellence, or, by a more conscientious adherence to what they aim at, rise superior.

[20] Sc. the Lacedaemonians. See W. L. Newman, op. cit. i. 396.

You would seem to suggest (he answered) that the spirit of beautiful and brave manhood has taken wings and left our city;[21] as, for instance, when will Athenians, like the Lacedaemonians, reverence old age - the Athenian, who takes his own father as a starting-point for the contempt he pours upon grey hairs? When will he pay as strict an attention to the body, who is not content with neglecting a good habit,[22] but laughs to scorn those who are careful in this matter? When shall we Athenians so obey our magistrates - we who take a pride, as it were, in despising authority? When, once more, shall we be united as a people - we who, instead of combining to promote common interests, delight in blackening each other's characters,[23] envying one another more than we envy all the world besides; and - which is our worst failing - who, in private and public intercourse alike, are torn by dissension and are caught in a maze of litigation, and prefer to make capital out of our neighbour's difficulties rather than to render natural assistance? To make our conduct consistent, indeed, we treat our national interests no better than if they were the concerns of some foreign state; we make them bones of contention to wrangle over, and rejoice in nothing so much as in possessing means and ability to indulge these tastes. From this hotbed is engendered in the state a spirit of blind folly[24] and cowardice, and in the hearts of the citizens spreads a tangle of hatred and mutual hostility which, as I often shudder to think, will some day cause some disaster to befall the state greater than it can bear.[25]

[21] Or, "is far enough away from Athens."
[22] See below, III. xii. 5; "Pol. Ath." i. 13; "Rev." iv. 52.
[23] Or, "to deal despitefully with one another.
[24] Reading {ateria}. See L. Dindorf ad loc., Ox. ed. lxii. Al. {apeiria}, a want of skill, or {ataxia}, disorderliness. Cf. "Pol. Ath." i. 5.
[25] Possibly the author is thinking of the events of 406, 405 B.C. (see "Hell." I. vii. and II.), and history may repeat itself.

Do not (replied Socrates), do not, I pray you, permit yourself to believe that Athenians are smitten with so incurable a depravity. Do you not observe their discipline in all naval matters? Look at their prompt and orderly obedience to the superintendents at the gymnastic contests,[26] their quite unrivalled subservience to their teachers in the training of our choruses.

[26] Epistatoi, i.e. stewards and training-masters.

Yes (he answered), there's the wonder of it; to think that all those good people should so obey their leaders, but that our hoplites and our cavalry, who may be supposed to rank before the rest of the citizens in excellence of manhood,[27] should be so entirely unamenable to discipline.

[27] {kalokagathia}.

Then Socrates: Well, but the council which sits on Areopagos is composed of citizens of approved[28] character, is it not?

[28] Technically, they must have passed the {dokimasia}. And for the "Aeropagos" see Grote, "H. G." v. 498; Aristot. "Pol." ii. 12; "Ath. Pol." 4. 4, where see Dr. Sandys' note, p. 18.

Certainly (he answered).

Soc. Then can you name any similar body, judicial or executive, trying cases or transacting other business with greater honour, stricter legality, higher dignity, or more impartial justice?

No, I have no fault to find on that score (he answered).

Soc. Then we ought not to despair as though all sense of orderliness and good discipline had died out of our countrymen.

Still (he answered), if it is not to harp upon one string, I maintain that in military service, where, if anywhere, sobriety and temperance, orderliness and good discipline are needed, none of these essentials receives any attention.

May it not perhaps be (asked Socrates) that in this department they are officered by those who have the least knowledge?[29] Do you not notice, to take the case of harp-players, choric performers, dancers, and the like, that no one would ever dream of leading if he lacked the requisite knowledge? and the same holds of wrestlers or pancratiasts.

[29] {episteme}. See below, III. ix. 10.

Moreover, while in these cases any one in command can tell you where he got the elementary knowledge of what he presides over, most generals are amateurs and improvisers.[30] I do not at all suppose that you are one of that sort. I believe you could give as clear an account of your schooling in strategy as you could in the matter of wrestling. No doubt you have got at first hand many of your father's "rules for generalship," which you carefully preserve, besides having collected many others from every quarter whence it was possible to pick up any knowledge which would be of use to a future general. Again, I feel sure you are deeply concerned to escape even unconscious ignorance of anything which will be serviceable to you in so high an office; and if you detect in yourself any ignorance, you turn to those who have knowledge in these matters (sparing neither gifts nor gratitude) to supplement your ignorance by their knowledge and to secure their help.

[30] Cf. "Pol. Lac." xiii. 5.

To which Pericles: I am not so blind, Socrates, as to imagine you say these words under the idea that I am truly so careful in these matters; but rather your object is to teach me that the would-be general must make such things his care. I admit in any case all you say.

Socrates proceeded: Has it ever caught your observation, Pericles, that a high mountain barrier stretches like a bulwark in front of our country down towards Boeotia - cleft, moreover, by narrow and precipitous passes, the only avenues into the heart of Attica, which lies engirdled by a ring of natural fortresses?[31]

[31] The mountains are Cithaeron and Parnes N., and Cerata N.W.

Per. Certainly I have.

Soc. Well, and have you ever heard tell of the Mysians and Pisidians living within the territory of the great king,[32] who, inside their mountain fortresses, lightly armed, are able to rush down and inflict much injury on the king's territory by their raids, while preserving their own freedom?

[32] For this illustration see "Anab." III. ii. 23; cf. "Econ." iv. 18, where Socrates ({XS}) refers to Cyrus's expedition and death.

Per. Yes, the circumstance is not new to me.

And do you not think (added Socrates) that a corps of young able- bodied Athenians, accoutred with lighter arms,[33] and holding our natural mountain rampart in possession, would prove at once a thorn in the enemy's side offensively, whilst defensively they would form a splendid bulwark to protect the country?

[33] Cf. the reforms of Iphicrates.

To which Pericles: I think, Socrates, these would be all useful measures, decidedly.

If, then (replied Socrates), these suggestions meet your approbation, try, O best of men, to realise them - if you can carry out a portion of them, it will be an honour to yourself and a blessing to the state; while, if you fail in any point, there will be no damage done to the city nor discredit to yourself.

VI

Glaucon,[1] the son of Ariston, had conceived such an ardour to gain the headship of the state that nothing could hinder him but he must deliver a course of public speeches,[2] though he had not yet reached the age of twenty. His friends and relatives tried in vain to stop him making himself ridiculous and being dragged down from the bema.[3] Socrates, who took a kindly interest in the youth for the sake of Charmides[4] the son of Glaucon, and of Plato, alone succeeded in restraining him. It happened thus. He fell in with him, and first of all, to get him to listen, detained him by some such remarks as the following:[5]

[1] Glaucon, Plato's brother. Grote, "Plato," i. 508.
[2] "Harangue the People."
[3] See Plat. "Protag." 319 C: "And if some person offers to give them advice who is not supposed by them to have any skill in the art [sc. of politics], even though he be good-looking, and rich, and noble, they will not listen to him, but laugh at him, and hoot him, until he is either clamoured down and retires of himself; or if he persists, he is dragged away or put out by the constables at the command of the prytanes" (Jowett). Cf. Aristoph. "Knights," 665, {kath eilkon auton oi prutaneis kai toxotai}.
    [4] For Charmides (maternal uncle of Plato and Glaucon, cousin of Critias) see ch. vii. below; Plato the philosopher, Glaucon's brother, see Cobet, "Pros. Xen." p. 28.
    [5] Or, "and in the first instance addressing him in such terms he could not choose but hear, detained him." See above, II. vi. 11. Socrates applies his own theory.

Ah, Glaucon (he exclaimed), so you have determined to become prime minister?[6]

[6] {prostateuein}.

Glauc. Yes, Socrates, I have.

Soc. And what a noble aim! if aught human ever deserved to be called noble; since if you succeed in your design, it follows, as the night the day, you will be able not only to gratify your every wish, but you will be in a position to benefit your friends, you will raise up your father's house, you will exalt your fatherland, you will become a name thrice famous in the city first, and next in Hellas, and lastly even among barbarians perhaps, like Themistocles; but be it here or be it there, wherever you be, you will be the observed of all beholders.[7]

[7] "The centre of attraction - the cynosure of neighbouring eyes."

The heart of Glaucon swelled with pride as he drank in the words, and gladly he stayed to listen.

Presently Socrates proceeded: Then this is clear, Glaucon, is it not? that you must needs benefit the city, since you desire to reap her honours?

Glauc. Undoubtedly.

Then, by all that is sacred (Socrates continued), do not keep us in the dark, but tell us in what way do you propose first to benefit the state? what is your starting-point?[8] When Glaucon remained with sealed lips, as if he were now for the first time debating what this starting-point should be, Socrates continued: I presume, if you wished to improve a friend's estate, you would endeavour to do so by adding to its wealth, would you not? So here, maybe, you will try to add to the wealth of the state?

[8] Or, "tell us what your starting-point will be in the path of benefaction."

Most decidedly (he answered).

Soc. And we may take it the state will grow wealthier in proportion as her revenues increase?

Glauc. That seems probable, at any rate.

Soc. Then would you kindly tell us from what sources the revenues of the state are at present derived, and what is their present magnitude? No doubt you have gone carefully into the question, so that if any of these are failing you may make up the deficit, or if neglected for any reason, make some new provision.[9]

[9] Or, "or if others have dropped out or been negligently overlooked, you may replace them."

Glauc. Nay, to speak the truth, these are matters I have not thoroughly gone into.

Never mind (he said) if you have omitted the point; but you might oblige us by running through the items or heads of expenditure. Obviously you propose to remove all those which are superfluous?

Glauc. Well, no. Upon my word I have not had time to look into that side of the matter either as yet.

Soc. Then we will postpone for the present the problem of making the state wealthier; obviously without knowing the outgoings and the incomings it would be impossible to deal with the matter seriously.

But, Socrates (Glaucon remarked), it is possible to enrich the state out of the pockets of her enemies!

Yes, to be sure, considerably (answered Socrates), in the event of getting the better of them; but in the event of being worsted, it is also possible to lose what we have got.

A true observation (he replied).

And therefore (proceeded Socrates), before he makes up his mind with what enemy to go to war, a statesman should know the relative powers of his own city and the adversary's, so that, in case the superiority be on his own side, he may throw the weight of his advice into the scale of undertaking war; but if the opposite he may plead in favour of exercising caution.

You are right (he answered).

Soc. Then would you for our benefit enumerate the land and naval forces first of Athens and then of our opponents?

Glauc. Pardon me. I could not tell you them off-hand at a moment's notice.

Or (added Socrates), if you have got the figures on paper, you might produce them. I cannot tell how anxious I am to hear your statement.

Glauc. No, I assure you, I have not got them even on paper yet.

Soc. Well then, we will defer tending advice on the topic of peace or war, in a maiden speech at any rate.[10] I can understand that, owing to the magnitude of the questions, in these early days of your ministry you have not yet fully examined them. But come, I am sure that you have studied the defences of the country, at all events, and you know exactly how many forts and outposts are serviceable[11] and how many are not; you can tell us which garrisons are strong enough and which defective; and you are prepared to throw in the weight of your advice in favour of increasing the serviceable outposts and sweeping away those that are superfluous?

[10] See "Econ." xi. 1.
[11] Or, "advantageously situated." See the author's own tract on "Revenues."

Glauc. Yes, sweep them all away, that's my advice; for any good that is likely to come of them! Defences indeed! so maintained that the property of the rural districts is simply pilfered.

But suppose you sweep away the outposts (he asked), may not something worse, think you, be the consequence? will not sheer plundering be free to any ruffian who likes? . . . But may I ask is this judgment the result of personal inspection? have you gone yourself and examined the defences? or how do you know that they are all maintained as you say?

Glauc. I conjecture that it is so.

Soc. Well then, until we have got beyond the region of conjecture shall we defer giving advice on the matter? (It will be time enough when we know the facts.)

Possibly it would be better to wait till then (replied Glaucon).

Soc. Then there are the mines,[12] but, of course, I am aware that you have not visited them in person, so as to be able to say why they are less productive than formerly.

[12] Again the author's tract on "Revenues" is a comment on the matter.

Well, no; I have never been there myself (he answered).

Soc. No, Heaven help us! an unhealthy district by all accounts; so that, when the moment for advice on that topic arrives, you will have an excuse ready to hand.

I see you are making fun of me (Glaucon answered).

Soc. Well, but here is a point, I am sure, which you have not neglected. No, you will have thoroughly gone into it, and you can tell us. For how long a time could the corn supplies from the country districts support the city? how much is requisite for a single year, so that the city may not run short of this prime necessary, before you are well aware; but on the contrary you with your full knowledge will be in a position to give advice on so vital a question, to the aid or may be the salvation of your country?

It is a colossal business this (Glaucon answered), if I am to be obliged to give attention to all these details.

Soc. On the other hand, a man could not even manage his own house or his estate well, without, in the first place, knowing what he requires, and, in the second place, taking pains, item by item, to supply his wants. But since this city consists of more than ten thousand houses, and it is not easy to pay minute attention to so many all at once, how is it you did not practise yourself by trying to augment the resources of one at any rate of these - I mean your own uncle's? The service would not be thrown away. Then if your strength suffices in the single case you might take in hand a larger number; but if you fail to relieve one, how could you possibly hope to succeed with many? How absurd for a man, if he cannot carry half a hundredweight, to attempt to carry a whole![13]

[13] Lit. "a single talent's weight . . . to carry two."

Glauc. Nay, for my part, I am willing enough to assist my uncle's house, if my uncle would only be persuaded to listen to my advice.

Soc. Then, when you cannot persuade your uncle, do you imagine you will be able to make the whole Athenian people, uncle and all, obey you? Be careful, Glaucon (he added), lest in your thirst for glory and high repute you come to the opposite. Do you not see how dangerous it is for a man to speak or act beyond the range[14] of his knowledge? To take the cases known to you of people whose conversation or conduct clearly transcends these limits: should you say they gain more praise or more blame on that account? Are they admired the rather or despised? Or, again, consider those who do know what they say and what they do; and you will find, I venture to say, that in every sort of undertaking those who enjoy repute and admiration belong to the class of those endowed with the highest knowledge; whilst conversely the people of sinister reputation, the mean and the contemptible, emanate from some depth of ignorance and dulness. If therefore what you thirst for is repute and admiration as a statesman, try to make sure of one accomplishment: in other words, the knowledge as far as in you lies of what you wish to do.[15] If, indeed, with this to distinguish you from the rest of the world you venture to concern yourself with state affairs, it would not surprise me but that you might reach the goal of your ambition easily.

[14] Or, "to talk of things which he does not know, or to meddle with them."
[15] Or, "try as far as possible to achieve one thing, and that is to know the business which you propose to carry out."

VII

Now Charmides,[1] the son of Glaucon, was, as Socrates observed, a man of mark and influence: a much more powerful person in fact than the mass of those devoted to politics at that date, but at the same time he was a man who shrank from approaching the people or busying himself with the concerns of the state. Accordingly Socrates addressed him thus:

[1] See last chapter for his relationship to Glaucon (the younger) and Plato; for a conception of his character, Plato's dialogue "Charmides"; "Theag." 128 E; "Hell." II. iv. 19; "Symp." iv. 31; Grote, "Plato," i. 480.

Tell me, Charmides, supposing some one competent to win a victory in the arena and to receive a crown,[2] whereby he will gain honour himself and make the land of his fathers more glorious in Hellas, [3] were to refuse to enter the lists - what kind of person should you set him down to be?

[2] In some conquest (e.g. of the Olympic games) where the prize is a mere wreath.
[3] Cf. Pindar passim.

Clearly an effeminate and cowardly fellow (he answered).
Soc. And what if another man, who had it in him, by devotion to affairs of state, to exalt his city and win honour himself thereby, were to shrink and hesitate and hang back - would he too not reasonably be regarded as a coward?
Possibly (he answered); but why do you address these questions to me?
Because (replied Socrates) I think that you, who have this power, do hesitate to devote yourself to matters which, as being a citizen, if for no other reason, you are bound to take part in.[4]

[4] Or add, "and cannot escape from."

Charm. And wherein have you detected in me this power, that you pass so severe a sentence upon me?
Soc. I have detected it plainly enough in those gatherings[5] in which you meet the politicians of the day, when, as I observe, each time they consult you on any point you have always good advice to offer,

and when they make a blunder you lay your finger on the weak point immediately.

[5] See above, I. v. 4; here possibly of political club conversation.

Charm. To discuss and reason in private is one thing, Socrates, to battle in the throng of the assembly is another.

Soc. And yet a man who can count, counts every bit as well in a crowd as when seated alone by himself; and it is the best performer on the harp in private who carries off the palm of victory in public.

Charm. But do you not see that modesty and timidity are feelings implanted in man's nature? and these are much more powerfully present to us in a crowd than within the cirlce of our intimates.

Soc. Yes, but what I am bent on teaching you is that while you feel no such bashfulness and timidity before the wisest and strongest of men, you are ashamed of opening your lips in the midst of weaklings and dullards.[6] Is it the fullers among them of whom you stand in awe, or the cobblers, or the carpenters, or the coppersmiths, or the merchants, or the farmers, or the hucksters of the market-place exchanging their wares, and bethinking them how they are to buy this thing cheap, and to sell the other dear - is it before these you are ashamed, for these are the individual atoms out of which the Public Assembly is composed?[7] And what is the difference, pray, between your behaviour and that of a man who, being the superior of trained athletes, quails before a set of amateurs? Is it not the case that you who can argue so readily with the foremost statesmen in the city, some of whom affect to look down upon you - you, with your vast superiority over practised popular debaters - are no sooner confronted with a set of folk who never in their lives gave politics a thought, and into whose heads certainly it never entered to look down upon you - than you are afraid to open your lips in mortal terror of being laughed at?

[6] Cf. Cic. "Tusc." v. 36, 104; Plat. "Gorg." 452 E, 454 B.
[7] Cf. Plat. "Protag." 319 C. See W. L. Newman, op. cit. i. 103.

Well, but you would admit (he answered) that sound argument does frequently bring down the ridicule of the Popular Assembly.

Soc. Which is equally true of the others.[8] And that is just what rouses my astonishment, that you who can cope so easily with these lordly people (when guilty of ridicule) should persuade yourself that you cannot stand up against a set of commoners.[9] My good fellow, do not be ignorant of yourself![10] do not fall into that commonest of errors - theirs who rush off to investigate the concerns of the rest of the world, and have no time to turn and examine themselves. Yet that is a duty which you must not in cowardly sort draw back from: rather must you brace ourself to give good heed to your own self; and as to public affairs, if by any manner of means they may be improved through you, do not neglect them. Success in the sphere of politics means that not only the mass of your fellow-citizens, but your personal friends and you yourself last but not least, will profit by your action.

[8] {oi eteroi}, i.e. "the foremost statesmen" mentioned before. Al. "the opposite party," the "Tories,"
if one may so say, of the political clubs.
[9] Lit. "those . . . these."
[10] Ernesti aptly cf. Cic. "ad Quint." iii. 6. See below, III. ix. 6; IV. ii. 24.

VIII

Once when Aristippus[1] set himself to subject Socrates to a cross- examination, such as he had himself undergone at the hands of Socrates on a former occasion,[2] Socrates, being minded to benefit those who were with him, gave his answers less in the style of a debater guarding against perversions of his argument, than of a man persuaded of the supreme importance of right conduct.[3]

[1] For Aristippus see above, p. 38; for the connection, {boulomenos tous sunontas ophelein}, between this and the preceeding chapter, see above, Conspectus, p. xxvi.

[2] Possibly in reference to the conversation above. In reference to the present dialogue see Grote, "Plato," I. xi. p. 380 foll.

[3] For {prattein ta deonta} cf. below, III. ix. 4, 11; Plat. "Charm." 164 B; but see J. J. Hartman, "An. Xen." p. 141.

Aristippus asked him "if he knew of anything good,"[4] intending in case he assented and named any particular good thing, like food or drink, or wealth, or health, or strength, or courage, to point out that the thing named was sometimes bad. But he, knowing that if a thing troubles us, we immediately want that which will put an end to our trouble, answered precisely as it was best to do.[5]

[4] See Grote, "Plato," ii. 585, on Philebus.
[5] Or, "made the happiest answer."

Soc. Do I understand you to ask me whether I know anything good for fever?
No (he replied), that is not my question.
Soc. Then for inflammation of the eyes?
Aristip. No, nor yet that.
Soc. Well then, for hunger?
Aristip. No, nor yet for hunger.
Well, but (answered Socrates) if you ask me whether I know of any good thing which is good for nothing, I neither know of it nor want to know.
And when Aristippus, returning to the charge, asked him "if he knew of any thing beautiful,"
He answered: Yes, many things.
Aristip. Are they all like each other?
Soc. On the contrary, they are often as unlike as possible.
How then (he asked) can that be beautiful which is unlike the beautiful?
Soc. Bless me! for the simple reason that it is possible for a man who is a beautiful runner to be quite unlike another man who is a beautiful boxer,[6] or for a shield, which is a beautiful weapon for the purpose of defence, to be absolutely unlike a javelin, which is a beautiful weapon of swift and sure discharge.

[6] See Grote, "H. G." x. 164, in reference to Epaminondas and his gymnastic training; below, III. x. 6.

Aristip. Your answers are no better now than[7] when I asked you whether you knew any good thing. They are both of a pattern.

[7] Or, "You answer precisely as you did when . . ."

Soc. And so they should be. Do you imagine that one thing is good and another beautiful? Do not you know that relatively to the same standard all things are at once beautiful and good?[8] In the first place, virtue is not a good thing relatively to one standard and a beautiful thing relatively to another standard; and in the next place, human beings, on the same principle[9] and relatively to the same standard, are called "beautiful and good"; and so the bodily frames of men relatively to the same standards are seen to be "beautiful and good," and in general all things capable of being used by man are regarded as at once beautiful and good relatively to the same standard - the standing being in each case what the thing happens to be useful for.[10]

[8] Or, "good and beautiful are convertible terms: whatever is good is beautiful, or whatever is beautiful is good."
[9] Or, "in the same breath." Cf. Plat. "Hipp. maj." 295 D; "Gorg." 474 D.
[10] Or, "and this standard is the serviceableness of the thing in question."
Aristip. Then I presume even a basket for carrying dung[11] is a beautiful thing?
[11] Cf. Plat. "Hipp. maj." 288 D, 290 D; and Grote's note, loc. cit. p. 381: "in regard to the question wherein consists {to kalon}?"

Soc. To be sure, and a spear of gold an ugly thing, if for their respective uses - the former is well and the latter ill adapted.

Aristip. Do you mean to assert that the same things may be beautiful and ugly?

Soc. Yes, to be sure; and by the same showing things may be good and bad: as, for instance, what is good for hunger may be bad for fever, and what is good for fever bad for hunger; or again, what is beautiful for wrestling is often ugly for running; and in general everything is good and beautiful when well adapted for the end in view, bad and ugly when ill adapted for the same.

Similarly when he spoke about houses,[12] and argued that "the same house must be at once beautiful and useful" - I could not help feeling that he was giving a good lesson on the problem: "how a house ought to be built." He investigated the matter thus:

[12] See K. Joel, op. cit. p. 488; "Classical Review," vii. 262.

Soc. "Do you admit that any one purposing to build a perfect house[13] will plan to make it at once as pleasant and as useful to live in as possible?" and that point being admitted,[14] the next question would be:

[13] Or, "the ideal house"; lit. "a house as it should be."
[14] See below, IV. vi. 15.

"It is pleasant to have one's house cool in summer and warm in winter, is it not?" and this proposition also having obtained assent, "Now, supposing a house to have a southern aspect, sunshine during winter will steal in under the verandah,[15] but in summer, when the sun traverses a path right over our heads, the roof will afford an agreeable shade, will it not? If, then, such an arrangement is desirable, the southern side of a house should be built higher to catch the rays of the winter sun, and the northern side lower to prevent the cold winds finding ingress; in a word, it is reasonable to suppose that the pleasantest and most beautiful dwelling place will be one in which the owner can at all seasons of the year find the pleasantest retreat, and stow away his goods with the greatest security."

[15] Or, "porticoes" or "collonades."

Paintings[16] and ornamental mouldings are apt (he said) to deprive one of more joy[17] than they confer.

[16] See "Econ." ix. 2; Plat. "Hipp. maj." 298 A; "Rep." 529; Becker, "Charicles," 268 (Engl. trans.)
[17] {euphrosunas}, archaic or "poetical" = "joyance." See "Hiero," vi. 1.

The fittest place for a temple or an altar (he maintained) was some site visible from afar, and untrodden by foot of man:[18] since it was a glad thing for the worshipper to lift up his eyes afar off and offer up his orison; glad also to wend his way peaceful to prayer unsullied.[19]

[18] e.g. the summit of Lycabettos, or the height on which stands the temple of Phygaleia. Cf. Eur. "Phoen." 1372, {Pallados khrusaspidos blepsas pros oikon euxato} of Eteocles.
[19] See Vitruvius, i. 7, iv. 5, ap. Schneid. ad loc.; W. L. Newman, op. cit. i. 338.

IX

Being again asked by some one: could courage be taught,[1] or did it come by nature? he answered: I imagine that just as one body is by nature stronger than another body to encounter toils, so one soul by nature grows more robust than another soul in face of dangers. Certainly I do note that people brought up under the same condition of laws and customs differ greatly in respect of daring. Still my belief is that by learning and practice the natural aptitude may always be strengthened towards courage. It is clear, for instance, that Scythians or Thracians would not venture to take shield and spear and contend with Lacedaemonians; and it is equally evident that Lacedaemonians would demur to entering the lists of battle against Thracians if limited to their light shields and javelins, or against Scythians without some weapon more familiar than their bows and arrows.[2] And as far as I can see, this principle holds generally: the natural differences of one man from another may be compensated by artificial progress, the result of care and attention. All which proves clearly that whether nature has endowed us with keener or blunter sensibilities, the duty of all alike is to learn and practise those things in which we would fain achieve distinction.

[1] Or, "When some one retorted upon him with the question: 'Can courage be taught?'" and for this problem see IV. vi. 10, 11; "Symp." ii. 12; Plat. "Lach."; "Protag." 349; "Phaedr." 269 D; K. Joel, op. cit. p. 325 foll.; Grote, "Plato," i. 468 foll., ii. 60; Jowett, "Plato," i. 77, 119; Newman, op. cit. i. 343.
[2] Or, "against Thracians with light shields and javelins, or against Scythians with bows and arrows"; and for the national arms of these peoples respectively see Arist. "Lysistr." 563; "Anab." III. iv. 15; VI. VII. Passim.

Between wisdom and sobriety of soul (which is temperance) he drew no distinction.[3] Was a man able on the one hand to recognise things beautiful and good sufficiently to live in them? Had he, on the other hand, knowledge of the "base and foul" so as to beware of them? If so, Socrates judged him to be wise at once and sound of soul (or temperate).[4]

[3] But cf. IV. vi. 7; K. Joel, op. cit. p. 363.
[4] Reading {alla to . . . kai to}, or more lit. "he discovered the wise man and sound of soul in his power not only to recognise things 'beautiful and good,' but to live and move and have his being in them; as also in his gift of avoiding consciously things base." Or if {alla ton . . . kai ton . . .} transl. "The man who not only could recognise the beautiful and good, but lived, etc., in that world, and who morever consciously avoided things base, in the judgment of Socrates was wise and sound of soul." Cf. Plat. "Charm."

And being further questioned whether "he considered those who have the knowledge of right action, but do not apply it, to be wise and self- controlled?" - "Not a whit more," he answered, "than I consider them to be unwise and intemperate.[5] Every one, I conceive, deliberately chooses what, within the limits open to him, he considers most conducive to his interest, and acts accordingly. I must hold therefore that those who act against rule and crookedly[6] are neither wise nor self-controlled.

[5] For the phrase "not a whit the more" see below, III. xii. 1; "Econ." xii. 18. Al. "I should by no means choose to consider them wise and self-controlled rather than foolish and intemperate."
[6] "Who cannot draw a straight line, ethically speaking."

He said that justice, moreover, and all other virtue is wisdom. That is to say, things just, and all things else that are done with virtue, are "beautiful and good"; and neither will those who know these things deliberately choose aught else in their stead, nor will he who lacks the special knowledge of them be able to do them, but even if he makes the attempt he will miss the mark and fail. So the wise alone can perform the things which are "beautiful and good"; they that are unwise cannot, but even if they try they fail. Therefore, since all things just, and generally all things "beautiful and good," are wrought with virtue, it is clear that justice and all other virtue is wisdom.

On the other hand, madness (he maintained) was the opposite to wisdom; not that he regarded simple ignorance as madness,[7] but he put it thus: for a man to be ignorant of himself, to imagine and suppose that he knows what he knows not, was (he argued), if not madness itself, yet something very like it. The mass of men no doubt hold a different language: if a man is all abroad on some matter of which the mass of mankind are ignorant, they do not pronounce him "mad";[8] but a like aberration of mind, if only it be about matters within the scope of ordinary knowledge, they call madness. For instance, any one who imagined himself too tall to pass under a gateway of the Long Wall without stooping, or so strong as to try to lift a house, or to attempt any other obvious impossibility, is a madman according to them; but in the popular sense he is not mad, if his obliquity is confined to small matters. In fact, just as strong desire goes by the name of passion in popular parlance, so mental obliquity on a grand scale is entitled madness.

[7] See K. Joel, op. cit. p. 346; Grote, "Plato," i. 400.
[8] Or, "they resent the term 'mad' being applied to people who are all abroad," etc. See Comte, "Pos. Pol." i. 575; ii. 373 (Engl. Trans.)

In answer to the question: what is envy? he discovered it to be a certain kind of pain; not certainly the sorrow felt at the misfortunes of a friend or the good fortune of an enemy - that is not envy; but, as he said, "envy is felt by those alone who are annoyed at the successes of their friends." And when some one or other expressed astonishment that any one friendlily disposed to another should be pained at his well-doing, he reminded him of a common tendency in people: when any one is faring ill their sympathies are touched, they rush to the aid of the unfortunate; but when fortune smiles on others, they are somwhow pained. "I do not say," he added, "this could happen to a thoughtful person; but it is no uncommon condition of a silly mind."[9]

[9] Or, "a man in his senses . . . a simpleton"; for the sentiment L. Dind. cf. Isocr. "ad Demonic." 7 D.

In answer to the question: what is leisure? I discover (he said) that most men do something:[10] for instance, the dice player,[11] the gambler, the buffoon, do something, but these have leisure; they can, if they like, turn and do something better; but nobody has leisure to turn from the better to the worse, and if he does so turn, when he has no leisure, he does but ill in that.

[10] See above, I. ii. 57; and in ref. to these definitions, K. Joel, op. cit. p. 347 foll.
[11] For "dice-playing" see Becker, "Charicl." 354 (Engl. trans.); for "buffoonery," ib. 98; "Symp."

(To pass to another definition.) They are not kings or rulers (he said) who hold the sceptre merely, or are chosen by fellows out of the street,[12] or are appointed by lot, or have stepped into office by violence or by fraud; but those who have the special knowledge[13] how to rule. Thus having won the admission that it is the function of a ruler to enjoin what ought to be done, and of those who are ruled to obey, he proceeded to point out by instances that in a ship the ruler or captain is the man of special knowledge, to whom, as an expert, the shipowner himself and all the others on board obey. So likewise, in the matter of husbandry, the proprietor of an estate; in that of sickness, the patient; in that of physical training of the body, the youthful athlete going through a course; and, in general, every one directly concerned in any matter needing attention and care will either attend to this matter personally, if he thinks he has the special knowledge; or, if he mistrusts his own science, will be eager to obey any expert on the spot, or will even send and fetch one from a distance. The guidance of this expert he will follow, and do what he has to do at his dictation.

[12] Tom, Dick, and Harry (as we say).
[13] The {episteme}. See above, III. v. 21; Newman, op. cit. i. 256.

And thus, in the art of spinning wool, he liked to point out that women are the rulers of men - and why? because they have the knowledge of the art, and men have not.

And if any one raised the objection that a tyrant has it in his power not to obey good and correct advice, he would retort: "Pray, how has he the option not to obey, considering the penalty hanging over him who disobeys the words of wisdom? for whatever the matter be in which he disobeys the word of good advice, he will fall into error, I presume, and falling into error, be punished." And to the suggestion that the tyrant could, if he liked, cut off the head of the man of wisdom, his answer was: "Do you think that he who destroys his best ally will go scot free, or suffer a mere slight and passing loss? Is he more likely to secure his salvation that way, think you, or to compass his own swift destruction?"[14]

[14] Or, "Is that to choose the path of safety, think you? Is it not rather to sign his own death-warrent?" L. Dind. cf. Hesiod, "Works and Days," 293. See Newman, op. cit. i. 393-397.

When some one asked him: "What he regarded as the best pursuit or business[15] for a man?" he answered: "Successful conduct";[16] and to a second question: "Did he then regard good fortune as an end to be pursued?" - "On the contrary," he answered, "for myself, I consider fortune and conduct to be diametrically opposed. For instance, to succeed in some desirable course of action without seeking to do so, I hold to be good fortune; but to do a thing well by dint of learning and practice, that according to my creed is successful conduct,[17] and those who make this the serious business of their life seem to me to do well."

[15] Or, "the noblest study."
[16] {eupraxia, eu prattein} - to do well, in the sense both of well or right doing, and of welfare, and is accordingly opposed to {eutukhia}, mere good luck or success. Cf. Plat. "Euthyd." 281 B.
[17] Lit. "well-doing"; and for the Socratic view see Newman, op. cit. i. 305, 401.

They are at once the best and the dearest in the sight of God[18] (he went on to say) who for instance in husbandry do well the things of farming, or in the art of healing all that belongs to healing, or in statecraft the affairs of state; whereas a man who does nothing well - nor well in anything - is (he added) neither good for anything nor dear to God.

[18] Or, "most divinely favoured." Cf. Plat. "Euthyphro," 7 A.

X

But indeed,[1] if chance brought him into conversation with any one possessed of an art, and using it for daily purposes of business, he never failed to be useful to this kind of person. For instance, stepping one time into the studio of Parrhasius[2] the painter, and getting into conversation with him -

[1] *{alla men kai} . . . "But indeed the sphere of his helpfulness was not circumscribed; if," etc.*
[2] *For Parrhasius of Ephesus, the son of Evenor and rival of Zeuxis, see Woltmann and Woermann, "Hist. of Painting," p. 47 foll.; Cobet, "Pros. Xen." p. 50 (cf. in particular Quint. XII. x. 627). At the date of conversation (real or ideal) he may be supposed to have been a young man.*

I suppose, Parrhasius (said he), painting may be defined as "a representation of visible objects," may it not?[3] That is to say, by means of colours and palette you painters represent and reproduce as closely as possible the ups and downs, lights and shadows, hard and soft, rough and smooth surfaces, the freshness of youth and the wrinkles of age, do you not?

[3] *Reading with Schneider, L. Dind., etc., after Stobaeus, {e graphike estin eikasia}, or if the vulg. {graphike estin e eikasia}, trans. "Painting is the term applied to a particular representation," etc.*

You are right (he answered), that is so.
Soc. Further, in portraying ideal types of beauty, seeing it is not easy to light upon any one human being who is absolutely devoid of blemish, you cull from many models the most beautiful traits of each, and so make your figures appear completely beautiful?[4]

[4] *Cf. Cic. "de Invent." ii. 1 ad in. of Zeuxis; Max. Tur. "Dissert." 23, 3, ap. Schneider ad loc.*

Parrh. Yes, that is how we do.[5]

[5] *Or, "that is the secret of our creations," or "our art of composition."*

Well, but stop (Socrates continued); do you also pretend to represent in similar perfection the characteristic moods of the soul, its captivating charm and sweetness, with its deep wells of love, its intensity of yearning, its burning point of passion? or is all this quite incapable of being depicted?
Nay (he answered), how should a mood be other than inimitable, Socrates, when it possesses neither linear proportion[6] nor colour, nor any of those qualities which you named just now; when, in a word, it is not even visible?

[6] *Lit. "symmetry." Cf. Plin. xxxv. 10, "primus symmetriam picturae dedit," etc.*

Soc. Well, but the kindly look of love, the angry glance of hate at any one, do find expression in the human subject, do they not?[7]

[7] *Or, "the glance of love, the scowl of hate, which one directs towards another, are recognised expressions of human feeling." Cf. the description of Parrhasius's own portrait of Demos, ap. Plin. loc. cit.*

Parrh. No doubt they do.
Soc. Then this look, this glance, at any rate may be imitated in the eyes, may it not?
Undoubtedly (he answered).

Soc. And do anxiety and relief of mind occasioned by the good or evil fortune of those we love both wear the same expression?

By no means (he answered); at the thought of good we are radiant, at that of evil a cloud hangs on the brow.

Soc. Then here again are looks with it is possible to represent?

Parrh. Decidedly.

Soc. Furthermore, as through some chink or crevice, there pierces through the countenance of a man, through the very posture of his body as he stands or moves, a glimpse of his nobility and freedom, or again of something in him low and grovelling - the calm of self-restraint, and wisdom, or the swagger of insolence and vulgarity?

You are right (he answered).

Soc. Then these too may be imitated?

No doubt (he said).

Soc. And which is the pleasanter type of face to look at, do you think - one on which is imprinted the characteristics of a beautiful, good, and lovable disposition, or one which bears the impress of what is ugly, and bad, and hateful?[8]

[8] For this theory cp. Ruskin, "Mod. P." ii. 94 foll. and indeed passim.

Parrh. Doubtless, Socrates, there is a vast distinction between the two.

At another time he entered the workshop of the sculptor Cleiton,[9] and in course of conversation with him said:

[9] An unknown artist. Coraes conj. {Kleona}. Cf. Plin. xxxiv. 19; Paus. v. 17, vi. 3. He excelled in portrait statues. See Jowett, "Plato," iv.; "Laws," p. 123.

You have a gallery of handsome people here,[10] Cleiton, runners, and wrestlers, and boxers, and pancratiasts - that I see and know; but how do you give the magic touch of life to your creations, which most of all allures the soul of the beholder through his sense of vision?

[10] Reading after L. Dind. {kaloi ous}, or if vulg. {alloious}, translate "You have a variety of types, Cleiton, not all of one mould, but runners," etc.; al. "I see quite well how you give the diversity of form to your runners," etc.

As Cleiton stood perplexed, and did not answer at once, Socrates added: Is it by closely imitating the forms of living beings that you succeed in giving that touch of life to your statues?

No doubt (he answered).

Soc. It is, is it not, by faithfully copying the various muscular contractions of the body in obedience to the play of gesture and poise, the wrinklings of flesh and the sprawl of limbs, the tensions and the relaxations, that you succeed in making your statues like real beings - make them "breathe" as people say?

Cleit. Without a doubt.

Soc. And does not the faithful imitation of the various affections of the body when engaged in any action impart a particular pleasure to the beholder?

Cleit. I should say so.

Soc. Then the threatenings in the eyes of warriors engaged in battle should be carefully copied, or again you should imitate the aspect of a conqueror radiant with success?

Cleit. Above all things.

Soc. It would seem then that the sculptor is called upon to incorporate in his ideal form the workings and energies also of the soul?

Paying a visit to Pistias,[11] the corselet maker, when that artist showed him some exquisite samples of his work, Socrates exclaimed:

[11] Cf. Athen. iv. 20, where the same artist is referred to apparently as {Piston}, and for the type of person see the "Portrait of a Tailor" by Moroni in the National Gallery - see "Handbook," Edw. T. Cook, p. 152.

By Hera! a pretty invention this, Pistias, by which you contrive that the corselet should cover the parts of the person which need protection, and at the same time leave free play to the arms and hands. . . . but tell me, Pistias (he added), why do you ask a higher price for these corselets of yours if they are not stouter or made of costlier material than the others?

Because, Socrates (he answered), mine are of much finer proportion.

Soc. Proportion! Then how do you make this quality apparent to the customer so as to justify the higher price - by measure or weight? For I presume you cannot make them all exactly equal and of one pattern - if you make them fit, as of course you do?

Fit indeed! that I most distinctly do (he answered), take my word for it: no use in a corselet without that.

But then are not the wearer's bodies themselves (asked Socrates) some well proportioned and others ill?

Decidedly so (he answered).

Soc. Then how do you manage to make the corselet well proportioned if it is to fit an ill-proportioned body?[12]

[12] Or, "how do you make a well-proportioned corselet fit an ill- proportioned body? how well proportioned?"

Pist. To the same degree exactly as I make it fit. What fits is well proportioned.

Soc. It seems you use the term "well-proportioned" not in an absolute sense, but in reference to the wearer, just as you might describe a shield as well proportioned to the individual it suits; and so of a military cloak, and so of the rest of things, in your terminology? But maybe there is another considerable advantage in this "fitting"?

Pist. Pray instruct me, Socrates, if you have got an idea.

Soc. A corselet which fits is less galling by its weight than one which does not fit, for the latter must either drag from the shoulders with a dead weight or press upon some other part of the body, and so it becomes troublesome and uncomfortable; but that which fits, having its weight distributed partly along the collar-bone and shoulder- blade, partly over the shoulders and chest, and partly the back and belly, feels like another natural integument rather than an extra load to carry.[13]

[13] Schneider ad loc. cf Eur. "Electr." 192, {prosthemata aglaias}, and for the weight cf. Aristoph. "Peace," 1224.

Pist. You have named the very quality which gives my work its exceptional value, as I consider; still there are customers, I am bound to say, who look for something else in a corselet - they must have them ornamental or inlaid with gold.

For all that (replied Socrates), if they end by purchasing an ill- fitting article, they only become the proprietors of a curiously- wrought and gilded nuisance, as it seems to me. But (he added), as the body is never in one fixed position, but is at one time curved, at another raised erect how can an exactly-modelled corselet fit?

Pist. It cannot fit at all.

You mean (Socrates continued) that it is not the exactly-modelled corselet which fits, but that which does not gall the wearer in the using?

Pist. There, Socrates, you have hit the very point. I see you understand the matter most precisely.[14]

[14] Or, "There, Socrates, you have hit the very phrase. I could not state the matter more explicitly myself."

XI

There was once in the city a fair woman named Theodote.[1] She was not only fair, but ready to consort with any suitor who might win her favour. Now it chanced that some one of the company mentioned her, saying that her beauty beggared description. "So fair is she," he added, "that painters flock to draw her portrait, to whom, within the limits of decorum, she displays the marvels of her beauty." "Then there is nothing for it but to go and see her," answered Socrates, "since to comprehend by hearsay what is beyond description is clearly impossible." Then he who had introduced the matter replied: "Be quick then to follow me"; and on this wise they set off to seek Theodote. They found her "posing" to a certain painter; and they took their stand as spectators. Presently the painter had ceased his work; whereupon Socrates:

[1] For Theodote see Athen. v. 200 F, xiii. 574 F; Liban. i. 582. Some say that it was Theodote who stood by Alcibiades to the last, though there are apparently other better claimants to the honour. Plut. "Alc." (Clough, ii. p. 50).

"Do you think, sirs, that we ought to thank Theodote for displaying her beauty to us, or she us for coming to gaze at her? . . . It would seem, would it not, that if the exhibition of her charms is the more profitable to her, the debt is on her side; but if the spectacle of her beauty confers the greater benefit on us, then we are her debtors."

Some one answered that "was an equitable statement of the case."

Well then (he continued), as far as she is concerned, the praise we bestow on her is an immediate gain; and presently, when we have spread her fame abroad, she will be further benefited; but for ourselves the immediate effect on us is a strong desire to touch what we have seen; by and by, too, we shall go away with a sting inside us, and when we are fairly gone we shall be consumed with longing. Consequently it seems that we should do her service and she accept our court.

Whereupon Theodote: Oh dear! if that is how the matter stands, it is I who am your debtor for the spectacle.[2]

[2] In reference to the remark of Socrates above; or, "have to thank you for coming to look at me."

At this point, seeing that the lady herself was expensively attired, and that she had with her her mother also, whose dress and style of attendance[3] were out of the common, not to speak of the waiting- women - many and fair to look upon, who presented anything but a forlorn appearance; while in every respect the whole house itself was sumptuously furnished - Socrates put a question:

[3] Or, "her mother there with her in a dress and general get-up ({therapeia}) which was out of the common." See Becker, "Charicles," p. 247 (Eng. tr.)

Pray tell me, Theodote, have you an estate in the country?

Theod. Not I indeed.

Soc. Then perhaps you possess a house and large revenues along with it?
Theod. No, nor yet a house.
Soc. You are not an employer of labour on a large scale?[4]

[4] Lit. "You have not (in your employ) a body of handicraftsmen of any sort?"

Theod. No, nor yet an employer of labour.
Soc. From what source, then, do you get your means of subsistence?[5]

[5] Or, Anglice, "derive your income."

Theod. My friends are my life and fortune, when they care to be kind to me.
Soc. By heaven, Theodote, a very fine property indeed, and far better worth possessing than a multitude of sheep or goats or cattle. A flock of friends! . . . But (he added) do you leave it to fortune whether a friend lights like a fly on your hand at random, or do you use any artifice[6] yourself to attract him?

[6] Or, "means and appliances," "machinery."

Theod. And how might I hit upon any artifice to attract him?
Soc. Bless me! far more naturally than any spider. You know how they capture the creatures on which they live;[7] by weaving webs of gossamer, is it not? and woe betide the fly that tumbles into their toils! They eat him up.

[7] Lit. "the creatures on which they live."

Theod. So then you would consel me to weave myself some sort of net?
Soc. Why, surely you do not suppose you are going to ensnare that noblest of all game - a lover, to wit - in so artless a fashion? Do you not see (to speak of a much less noble sort of game) what a number of devices are needed to bag a hare?[8] The creatures range for their food at night; therefore the hunter must provide himself with night dogs. At peep of dawn they are off as fast as they can run. He must therefore have another pack of dogs to scent out and discover which way they betake them from their grazing ground to their forms;[9] and as they are so fleet of foot that they run and are out of sight in no time, he must once again be provided with other fleet-footed dogs to follow their tracks and overtake them;[10] and as some of them will give even these the slip, he must, last of all, set up nets on the paths at the points of escape, so that they may fall into the meshes and be caught.

[8] See the author's own treatise on "Hunting," vi. 6 foll.
[9] Lit. "from pasture to bed."
[10] Or, "close at their heels and run them down." See "Hunting"; cf. "Cyrop." I. vi. 40.

Theod. And by what like contrivance would you have me catch my lovers?
Soc. Well now! what if in place of a dog you can get a man who will hunt up your wealthy lover of beauty and discover his lair, and having found him, will plot and plan to throw him into your meshes?
Theod. Nay, what sort of meshes have I?
Soc. One you have, and a close-folding net it is,[11] I trow; to wit, your own person; and inside it sits a soul that teaches you[12] with what looks to please and with what words to cheer; how, too, with smiles you are to welcome true devotion, but to exclude all wantons from your presence.[13] It tells you, you are to visit your beloved in sickness with solicitude, and when he has wrought some noble deed you

are greatly to rejoice with him; and to one who passionately cares for you, you are to make surrender of yourself with heart and soul. The secret of true love I am sure you know: not to love softly merely, but devotedly.[14] And of this too I am sure: you can convince your lovers of your fondness for them not by lip phrases, but by acts of love.

[11] Or, "right well woven."
[12] Lit. "by which you understand."
[13] Or, "with what smiles to lie in wait for (cf. 'Cyrop.' II. iv. 20; Herod. vi. 104) the devoted admirer, and how to banish from your presence the voluptary."
[14] Or, "that it should be simply soft, but full of tender goodwill."

Theod. No, upon my word, I have none of these devices.

Soc. And yet it makes all the difference whether you approach a human being in the natural and true way, since it is not by force certainly that you can either catch or keep a friend. Kindness and pleasure are the only means to capture this fearful wild-fowl man and keep him constant.

Theod. You are right.

Soc. In the first place you must make such demands only of your well- wisher as he can grant without repentance; and in the next place you must make requital, dispensing your favours with a like economy. Thus you will best make friends whose love shall last the longest and their generosity know no stint.[15] And for your favours you will best win your friends if you suit your largess to their penury; for, mark you, the sweetest viands presented to a man before he wants them are apt to prove insipid, or, to one already sated, even nauseous; but create hunger, and even coarser stuff seems honey-sweet.

[15] Or, "This is the right road to friendship - permanent and open- handed friendship."

Theod. How then shall I create this hunger in the heart of my friends?

Soc. In the first place you must not offer or make suggestion of your dainties to jaded appetites until satiety has ceased and starvation cries for alms. Even then shall you make but a faint suggestion to their want, with modest converse - like one who would fain bestow a kindness . . . and lo! the vision fades and she is gone - until the very pinch of hunger; for the same gifts have then a value unknown before the moment of supreme desire.

Then Theodote: Oh why, Socrates, why are you not by my side (like the huntsman's assistant) to help me catch my friends and lovers?

Soc. That will I be in good sooth if only you can woo and win me.

Theod. How shall I woo and win you?

Soc. Seek and you will find means, if you truly need me.

Theod. Come then in hither and visit me often.

And Socrates, poking sly fun at his own lack of business occupation, answered: Nay, Theodote, leisure is not a commodity in which I largely deal. I have a hundred affairs of my own too, private or public, to occupy me; and then there are my lady-loves, my dear friends, who will not suffer me day or night to leave them, for ever studying to learn love-charms and incantations at my lips.

Theod. Why, are you really versed in those things, Socrates?

Soc. Of course, or else how is it, do you suppose, that Apollodorus[16] here and Antisthenes never leave me; or why have Cebes and Simmias come all the way from Thebes to stay with me? Be assured these things cannot happen without diverse love-charms and incantations and magic wheels.

[16] For Apollodorus see "Apol." 28; Plat. "Symp." 172 A; "Phaed." 59 A, 117 D. For Antisthenes see above. For Cebes and Simmias see above, I. ii. 48; Plat. "Crit." 45 B; "Phaed." passim.

Theod. I wish you would lend me your magic-wheel,[17] then, and I will set it spinning first of all for you.

[17] Cf. Theocr. ii. 17; Schneider ad loc.

Soc. Ah! but I do not wish to be drawn to you. I wish you to come to me.

Theod. Then I will come. Only, will you be "at home" to me?

Soc. Yes, I will welcome you, unless some one still dearer holds me engaged, and I must needs be "not at home."

XII

Seeing one of those who were with him, a young man, but feeble of body, named Epigenes,[1] he addressed him.

[1] Epigenes, possibly the son of Antiphon. See Plat. "Apol." 33 E; "Phaed." 59 B.

Soc. You have not the athletic appearance of a youth in training,[2] Epigenes.

[2] {idiotikos}, lit. of the person untrained in gymnastics. See A. R. Cluer ad loc. Cf. Plat. "Laws," 839 E; I. ii. 4; III. v. 15; "Symp." ii. 17.

And he: That may well be, seeing I am an amateur and not in training.

Soc. As little of an amateur, I take it, as any one who ever entered the lists of Olympia, unless you are prepared to make light of that contest for life and death against the public foe which the Athenians will institute when the day comes.[3] And yet they are not a few who, owing to a bad habit of body, either perish outright in the perils of war, or are ignobly saved. Many are they who for the self-same cause are taken prisoners, and being taken must, if it so betide, endure the pains of slavery for the rest of their days; or, after falling into dolorous straits,[4] when they have paid to the uttermost farthing of all, or may be more than the worth of all, that they possess, must drag on a miserable existence in want of the barest necessaries until death release them. Many also are they who gain an evil repute through infirmity of body, being thought to play the coward. Can it be that you despise these penalties affixed to an evil habit? Do you think you could lightly endure them? Far lighter, I imagine, nay, pleasant even by comparison, are the toils which he will undergo who duly cultivates a healthy bodily condition. Or do you maintain that the evil habit is healthier, and in general more useful than the good? Do you pour contempt upon those blessings which flow from the healthy state? And yet the very opposite of that which befalls the ill attends the sound condition. Does not the very soundness imply at once health and strength?[5] Many a man with no other talisman than this has passed safely through the ordeal of war; stepping, not without dignity,[6] through all its horrors unscathed. Many with no other support than this have come to the rescue of friends, or stood forth as benefactors of their fatherland; whereby they were thought worthy of gratitude, and obtained a great renown and received as a recompense the highest honours of the State; to whom is also reserved a happier and brighter passage through what is left to them of life, and at their death they leave to their children the legacy of a fairer starting-point in the race of life.

[3] Or, "should chance betide." Is the author thinking of a life-and- death struggle with Thebes?

[4] e.g. the prisoners in the Latomiae. Thuc. vii. 87.

[5] It is almost a proverb - "Sound of body and limb is hale and strong." "Qui valet praevalebit."

[6] e.g. Socrates himself, according to Alcibiades, ap. Plat. "Symp." 221 B; and for the word

{euskhemonos} see Arist. "Wasps," 1210, "like a gentleman"; L. and S.; "Cyr." I. iii. 8; Aristot. "Eth. N." i. 10, 13, "gracefully."

Because our city does not practise military training in public,[7] that is no reason for neglecting it in private, but rather a reason for making it a foremost care. For be you assured that there is no contest of any sort, nor any transaction, in which you will be the worse off for being well prepared in body; and in fact there is nothing which men do for which the body is not a help. In every demand, therefore, which can be laid upon the body it is much better that it should be in the best condition; since, even where you might imagine the claims upon the body to be slightest - in the act of reasoning - who does not know the terrible stumbles which are made through being out of health? It suffices to say that forgetfulness, and despondency, and moroseness, and madness take occasion often of ill-health to visit the intellectual faculties so severely as to expel all knowledge[8] from the brain. But he who is in good bodily plight has large security. He runs no risk of incurring any such catastrophe through ill-health at any rate; he has the expectation rather that a good habit must procure consequences the opposite to those of an evil habit;[9] and surely to this end there is nothing a man in his senses would not undergo. . . . It is a base thing for a man to wax old in careless self-neglect before he has lifted up his eyes and seen what manner of man he was made to be, in the full perfection of bodily strength and beauty. But these glories are withheld from him who is guilty of self-neglect, for they are not wont to blaze forth unbidden.[10]

[7] Cf. "Pol. Ath." i. 13; and above, III. v. 15.

[8] Or, "whole branches of knowledge" ({tas epistemas}).

[9] Or, "he may well hope to be insured by his good habit against the evils attendant on its opposite."

[10] Or, "to present themselves spontaneously."

XII

Once when some one was in a fury of indignation because he had bidden a passer-by good-day and the salutation was not returned, Socrates said: "It is enough to make one laugh! If you met a man in a wretched condition of body, you would not fall into a rage; but because you stumble upon a poor soul somewhat boorishly disposed, you feel annoyed."

To the remark of another who complained that he did not take his foot with pleasure, he said: "Acumenus[1] has a good prescription for that." And when the other asked: "And what may that be?" "To stop eating," he said. "On the score of pleasure, economy, and health, total abstinence has much in its favour."[2]

[1] A well-known physician. See Plat. "Phaedr." 227 A, 269 A; "Symp." 176 B. A similar story is told of Dr. Abernethy, I think.

[2] Lit. "he would live a happier, thriftier, and healthier life, if he stopped eating."

And when some one else lamented that "the drinking-water in his house was hot," he replied: "Then when you want a warm bath you will not have to wait."

The Other. But for bathing purposes it is cold.

Soc. Do you find that your domestics seem to mind drinking it or washing in it?

The Other. Quite the reverse; it is a constant marvel to me how contentedly they use it for either purpose.

Soc. Which is hotter to the taste - the water in your house or the hot spring in the temple of Asclepius?[3]

[3] In the Hieron at Epidauros probably. See Baedeker, "Greece," p. 240 foll.

The Other. The water in the temple of Asclepius.
Soc. And which is colder for bathing - yours or the cold spring in the cave of Amphiaraus?[4]

[4] Possibly at Oropos. Cf. Paus. i. 34. 3.

The Other. The water in the cave of Amphiaraus.
Soc. Then please to observe: if you do not take care, they will set you down as harder to please than a domestic servant or an invalid.[5]

[5] i.e. "the least and the most fastidious of men."

A man had administered a severe whipping to the slave in attendance on him, and when Socrates asked: "Why he was so wroth with his own serving-man?" excused himself on the ground that "the fellow was a lazy, gourmandising, good-for-nothing dolt - fonder of money than of work." To which Socrates: "Did it ever strike you to consider which of the two in that case the more deserves a whipping - the master or the man?"

When some one was apprehending the journey to Olympia, "Why are you afraid of the long distance?" he asked. "Here at home you spend nearly all your day in taking walks.[6] Well, on your road to Olympia you will take a walk and breakfast, and then you will take another walk and dine, and go to bed. Do you not see, if you take and tack together five or six days' length of walks, and stretch them out in one long line, it will soon reach from Athens to Olympia? I would recommend you, however, to set off a day too soon rather than a day too late. To be forced to lengthen the day's journey beyond a reasonable amount may well be a nuisance; but to take one day's journey beyond what is necessary is pure relaxation. Make haste to start, I say, and not while on the road."[7]

[6] {peripateis}, "promenading up and down."
[7] "Festina lente" - that is your motto.

When some one else remarked "he was utterly prostrated after a long journey," Socrates asked him: "Had he had any baggage to carry?"
"Not I," replied the complainer; "only my cloak."
Soc. Were you travelling alone, or was your man-servant with you?
He. Yes, I had my man.
Soc. Empty-handed, or had he something to carry?
He. Of course; carrying my rugs and other baggage.
Soc. And how did he come off on the journey?
He. Better than I did myself, I take it.
Soc. Well, but now suppose you had had to carry his baggage, what would your condition have been like?
He. Sorry enough, I can tell you; or rather, I could not have carried it at all.
Soc. What a confession! Fancy being capable of so much less toil than a poor slave boy! Does that sound like the perfection of athletic training?

XIV

On the occasion of a common dinner-party[1] where some of the company would present themselves with a small, and others with a large supply of viands, Socrates would bid the servants[2] throw the small supplies into the general stock, or else to help each of the party to a share all round. Thus the grand victuallers were ashamed in the one case not to share in the common stock, and in the other not to throw in their supplies also.[3] Accordingly in went the grand supplies into the common stock. And now, being no better off than the small contributors, they soon ceased to cater for expensive delicacies.

[1] For the type of entertainment see Becker, "Charicles," p. 315 (Eng. tr.)

[2] "The boy."

[3] Or, "were ashamed not to follow suit by sharing in the common stock and contributing their own portion."

At a supper-party one member of the company, as Socrates chanced to note, had put aside the plain fare and was devoting himself to certain dainties.[4] A discussion was going on about names and definitions, and the proper applications of terms to things.[5] Whereupon Socrates, appealing to the company: "Can we explain why we call a man a 'dainty fellow'? What is the particular action to which the term applies?[6] - since every one adds some dainty to his food when he can get it.[7] But we have not quite hit the definition yet, I think. Are we to be called dainty eaters because we like our bread buttered?"[8]

[4] For the distinction between {sitos} and {opson} see Plat. "Rep." 372 C.

[5] Or, "The conversation had fallen upon names: what is the precise thing denoted under such and such a term? Define the meaning of so and so."

[6] {opsophagos} = {opson} (or relish) eater, and so a "gourmand" or "epicure"; but how to define a gourmand?

[7] Lit. "takes some {opson} (relish) to his {sitos} (food)."

[8] Lit. "simply for that" (sc. the taking of some sort of {opson}. For {epi touto} cf. Plat. "Soph." 218 C; "Parmen." 147 D.

No! hardly! (some member of the company replied).

Soc. Well, but now suppose a man confine himself to eating venison or other dainty without any plain food at all, not as a matter of training,[9] but for the pleasure of it: has such a man earned the title? "The rest of the world would have a poor chance against him,"[10] some one answered. "Or," interposed another, "what if the dainty dishes he devours are out of all proportion to the rest of his meal - what of him?"[11]

[9] Lit. "{opson} (relish) by itself, not for the sake of training," etc. The English reader wil bear in mind that a raw beefsteak or other meat prescribed by the gymnastic trainer in preference to farinaceous food ({sitos}) would be {opson}.

[10] Or, more lit. "Hardly any one could deserve the appellation better."

[11] Lit. "and what of the man who eats much {opson} on the top of a little ({sitos})?" {epesthion} = follows up one course by another, like the man in a fragment of Euripides, "Incert." 98: {kreasi boeiois khlora suk' epesthien}, who "followed up his beefsteak with a garnish of green figs."

Soc. He has established a very fair title at any rate to the appellation, and when the rest of the world pray to heaven for a fine harvest: "May our corn and oil increase!" he may reasonably ejaculate, "May my fleshpots multiply!"

At this last sally the young man, feeling that the conversation set somewhat in his direction, did not desist indeed from his savoury viands, but helped himself generously to a piece of bread. Socrates was all-observant, and added: Keep an eye on our friend yonder, you others next him, and see fair play between the sop and the sauce.[12]

[12] Lit. "see whether he will make a relish of the staple or a staple of the relish" ("butter his bread or bread his butter").

Another time, seeing one of the company using but one sop of bread[13] to test several savoury dishes, he remarked: Could there be a more extravagant style of cookery, or more murderous to the dainty dishes themselves, than this wholesale method of taking so many dishes together? - why, bless me, twenty different sorts of seasoning at one swoop![14] First of all he mixes up actually more ingredients than the cook himself prescribes, which is extravagant; and secondly, he has the audacity to commingle what the chef holds incongruous, whereby if the cooks are right in their method he is wrong in his, and consequently the destroyer of their art. Now is it not ridiculous first to procure the greatest virtuosi to cook for us, and then without any claim to their skill to take and alter their procedure? But there is a worse thing in store for the bold man who habituates himself to eat a dozen dishes at once: when there are but few dishes served, out of pure habit he will feel himself half starved, whilst his neighbour, accustomed to send his sop down by help of a single relish, will feast merrily, be the dishes never so few.

[13] {psomos}, a sop or morsel of bread (cf. {psomion}, N. T., in mod. Greek = "bread").
[14] Huckleberry Finn (p. 2 of that young person's "Adventures") propounds the rationale of the system: "In a barrel of odds and ends it is different; things get mixed up, and the juice kind of swaps around, and the things go better."

He had a saying that {euokheisthai}, to "make good cheer,"[15] was in Attic parlance a synonym for "eating," and the affix {eu} (the attributive "good") connoted the eating of such things as would not trouble soul or body, and were not far to seek or hard to find. So that to "make good cheer" in his vocabulary applied to a modest and well-ordered style of living.[16]

[15] {euokheisthai}, cf. "Cyrop." IV. v. 7; "Pol. Ath." ii. 9; Kuhner cf. Eustah. "ad Il." ii. p. 212, 37, {'Akhaioi ten trophen okhen legousin oxutonos}. Athen. viii. 363 B. See "Hipparch," viii. 4, of horses. Cf. Arist. "H. A." viii. 6.
[16] See "Symp." vi. 7; and for similar far-fetched etymologies, Plat. "Crat." passim.

BOOK IV

I

Such was Socrates; so helpful under all circumstances and in every way that no observer, gifted with ordinary sensibility, could fail to appreciate the fact, that to be with Socrates, and to spend long time in his society (no matter where or what the circumstances), was indeed a priceless gain. Even the recollection of him, when he was no longer present, was felt as no small benefit by those who had grown accustomed to be with him, and who accepted him. Nor indeed was he less helpful to his acquaintance in his lighter than in his graver moods.

Let us take as an example that saying of his, so often on his lips: "I am in love with so and so"; and all the while it was obvious the going-forth of his soul was not towards excellence of body in the bloom of beauty, but rather towards faculties of the soul unfolding in virtue.[1] And these "good natures" he detected by certain tokens: a readiness to learn that to which the attention was directed; a power of retaining in the memory the lessons learnt; and a passionate predilection for those studies in particular which serve to good administration of a house or of a state,[2] and in general to the proper handling of man and human affairs. Such beings, he maintained, needed only to be educated[3] to become not only happy themselves and happy administrators of their private households, but to be capable of rendering other human beings as states or individuals happy also.

[1] Or, "not excellence of body in respect of beauty, but of the soul as regards virtue; and this good natural disposition might be detected by the readiness of its possessor to learn," etc. Cf. Plat. "Rep." 535 B.

[2] Cf. above, I. i. 7.

[3] Or, "A person of this type would, if educated, not only prove a fortune-favoured invididual himself and," etc. Al. Kuhner, "Eos, qui ita instituti sunt, ut tales sint."

He had indeed a different way of dealing with different kinds of people.[4] Those who thought they had good natural ability and despised learning he instructed that the most highly-gifted nature stands most in need of training and education;[5] and he would point out how in the case of horses it is just the spirited and fiery thoroughbred which, if properly broken in as a colt, will develop into a serviceable and superb animal, but if left unbroken will turn out utterly intractable and good for nothing. Or take the case of dogs: a puppy exhibiting that zest for toil and eagerness to attack wild creatures which are the marks of high breeding,[6] will, if well brought up, prove excellent for the chase or for any other useful purpose; but neglect his education and he will turn out a stupid, crazy brute, incapable of obeying the simplest command. It is just the same with human beings; here also the youth of best natural endowments - that is to say, possessing the most robust qualities of spirit and a fixed determination to carry out whatever he has laid his hand to - will, if trained and taught what it is right to do, prove a superlatively good and useful man. He achieves, in fact, what is best upon the grandest scale. But leave him in boorish ignorance untrained, and he will prove not only very bad but very mischievous,[7] and for this reason, that lacking the knowledge to discern what is right to do, he will frequently lay his hand to villainous practices; whilst the very magnificence and vehemence of his character render it impossible either to rein him in or to turn him aside from his evil courses. Hence in his case also his achievements are on the grandest scale but of the worst.[8]

[4] Or, "His method of attack was not indeed uniformly the same. It varied with the individual."

[5] Or, "If any one was disposed to look down upon learning and study in reliance upon his own natural ability, he tried to lesson him that it is just the highly-gifted nature which stands," etc. See Newman, op. cit. i. 397.

[6] Cf. Aristot. "H. A." ix. 1; and "Hunting," iii. 11.

[7] Or, "and the same man may easily become a master villain of the most dangerous sort."

[8] Kuhner ad loc. after Fr. Hermann cf. Plato. "Crito," 44 E; "Hipp. min." 375 E; "Rep." vi. 491 E; "Gorg." 526 A; "Polit." 303 A.

Or to take the type of person so eaten up with the pride of riches that he conceives himself dispensed from any further need of education - since it is "money makes the man," and his wealth will amply suffice him to carry out his desires and to win honours from admiring humanity.[9] Socrates would bring such people to their senses by pointing out the folly of supposing that without instruction it was possible to draw the line of demarcation[10] between what is gainful and what is hurtful in conduct; and the further folly of supposing that, apart from such discrimination, a man could help himself by means of wealth alone to whatever he liked or find the path of expediency plain before him; and was it not the veriest simplicity to suppose that, without the power of labouring profitably, a man can either be doing well or be in any sort of way sufficiently equipped for the battle of life? and again, the veriest simplicity to suppose that by mere wealth without true knowledge it was possible either to purchase a reputation for some excellence, or without such reputation to gain distinction and celebrity?

[9] Or, "and to be honoured by mankind."

[10] Or, "that without learning the distinction it was possible to distinguish between," etc.

II

Or to come to a third kind - the class of people who are persuaded that they have received the best education, and are proud of their wisdom: his manner of dealing with these I will now describe.

Euthydemus[1] "the beautiful" had (Socrates was given to understand) collected a large library, consisting of the most celebrated poets and philosophers,[2] by help of which he already believed himself to be more than a match for his fellows in wisdom, and indeed might presently expect to out-top them all in capacity of speech and action.[3] At first, as Socrates noted, the young man by reason of his youth had not as yet set foot in the agora,[4] but if he had anything to transact, his habit was to seat himself in a saddler's shop hard by. Accordingly to this same saddler's shop Socrates betook himself with some of those who were with him. And first the question was started by some one: "Was it through consorting with the wise,[5] or by his own unaided talent, that Themistocles came so to surpass his fellow-citizens that when the services of a capable man were needed the eyes of the whole community instinctively turned to him?" Socrates, with a view to stirring[6] Euthydemus, answered: There was certainly an ingenuous simplicity in the belief that superiority in arts of comparatively little worth could only be attained by aid of qualified teachers, but that the leadership of the state, the most important concern of all, was destined to drop into the lap of anybody, no matter whom, like an accidental windfall.[7]

[1] Euthydemus, the son of Diocles perhaps. See Plat. "Symp." 222 B, and Jowet ad loc.; Cobet, "Prosop. Xen." s.n.; K. Joel, op. cit. p. 372 foll. For {ton kalon} cf. "Phaedr." 278 E, "Isocrates the fair." For the whole chapter cf. Plat. "Alc." i.; "Lys." 210 E. See above, "Mem." I. ii. 29; Grote, "Plato," i. ch. x. passim.

[2] Lit. "sophists." See Grote, "H. G." viii. p. 480, note. For private libraries see Becker, "Char." p. 272 foll. (Eng. tr.)

[3] See "Hipparch," i. 24; "Cyrop." V. v. 46.

[4] See above, III. vi. 1; Schneid. cf. Isocr. "Areop." 149 C.

[5] Cf. Soph. fr. 12, {sophoi turannoi ton sophon xunousia}.

[6] L. and S. cf. Plat. "Lys." 223 A; "Rep." 329 B: "Wishing to draw him out."

[7] Cf. Plat. "Alc." i. 118 C: "And Pericles is said not to have got his wisdom by the light of nature, but to have associated with several of the philosophers" (Jowett).

On a subsequent occasion, Euthydemus being present, though, as was plain to see, somewhat disposed to withdraw from the friendly concourse,[8] as if he would choose anything rather than appear to admire Socrates on the score of wisdom, the latter made the following remarks.

[8] {sunedrias}, "the council."

Soc. It is clear from his customary pursuits, is it not, sirs, that when our friend Euthydemus here is of full age, and the state propounds some question for solution, he will not abstain from offering the benefit of his advice? One can imagine the pretty exordium to his parliamentary speeches which, in his anxiety not to be thought to have learnt anything from anybody, he has ready for the occasion.[9] Clearly at the outset he will deliver himself thus: "Men of Athens, I have never at any time learnt anything from anybody; nor, if I have ever heard of any one as being an able statesman, well versed in speech and capable of action, have I sought to come across him individually. I have not so much as been at pains to provide muself with a teacher from amongst those who have knowledge;[10] on the contrary, I have persistently avoided, I will not say learning from others, but the very faintest suspicion of so doing. However, anything that occurs to me by the light of nature I shall be glad to place at your disposal." . . . How appropriate[11] would such a preface sound on the lips of any one seeking, say, the office of state physician,[12] would it not? How advantageously he might begin an address on this wise: "Men of Athens, I have never learnt the art of healing by help of anybody, nor have I sought to provide myself with any teacher among medical men. Indeed, to put it briefly, I have been ever on my guard not only against learning anything from the profession, but against the very notion of having studied medicine at all. If, however, you will be so good as to confer on me this post, I promise I will do my best to acquire skill by experimenting on your persons." Every one present laughed at the exordium (and there the matter dropped).

[9] Or, "the pretty exordium . . . now in course of conposition. He must at all hazards avoid the suspicion of having picked up any crumb of learning from anybody; how can he help therefore beginning his speech thus?"
[10] Or, "scientific experts."
[11] Al. "Just as if one seeking the office of state physician were to begin with a like exordium." {armoseie} = "it would be consistent (with what has gone before)."
[12] Schneider cf. Plat. "Laws," iv. 720 A; "Gorg." 456 A; and for "the parish doctor," "Polit." 259 A; Arist. "Acharn." 1030.

Presently, when it became apparent that Euthydemus had got so far that he was disposed to pay attention to what was said, though he was still at pains not to utter a sound himself, as if he hoped by silence to attach to himself some reputation for sagacity, Socrates, wishing to cure him of that defect, proceeded.

Soc. Is it not surprising that people anxious to learn to play the harp or the flute, or to ride, or to become proficient in any like accomplishment, are not content to work unremittingly in private by themselves at whatever it is in which they desire to excel, but they must sit at the feet of the best-esteemed teachers, doing all things and enduring all things for the sake of following the judgment of those teachers in everything, as though they themselves could not otherwise become famous; whereas, among those who aspire to become eminent politically as orators and statesmen,[13] there are some who cannot see why they should not be able to do all that politics demand, at a moment's notice, by inspiration as it were, without any preliminary pains or preparations whatever? And yet it would appear that the latter concerns must be more difficult of achievement than the former, in proportion as there are more competitors in the field but fewer who reach the goal of their ambition, which is as much as to say that a more sustained effort of attention is needed on the part of those who embark upon the sea of politics than is elsewhere called for.

[13] Or, more lit. "powerful in speech and action within the sphere of politics."

Such were the topics on which Socrates was wont in the early days of their association to dilate in the hearing of Euthydemus; but when the philosopher perceived that the youth not only could tolerate the turns of the discussion more readily but was now become a somewhat eager listener, he went to the saddler's shop alone,[14] and when Euthydemus was seated by his side the following conversation took place.

[14] The question arises: how far is the conversation historical or imaginary?

Soc. Pray tell me, Euthydemus, is it really true what people tell me, that you have made a large collection of the writings of "the wise," as they are called?[15]

[15] Or, "have collected several works of our classical authors and philosophers."

Euthydemus answered: Quite true, Socrates, and I mean to go on collecting until I possess all the books I can possibly lay hold of.
Soc. By Hera! I admire you for wishing to possess treasures of wisdom rather than of gold and silver, which shows that you do not believe gold and silver to be the means of making men better, but that the thoughts[16] of the wise alone enrich with virtue their possessions.

[16] Lit. "gnomes," maxims, sententiae. Cf. Aristot. "Rhet." ii. 21.

And Euthydemus was glad when he heard that saying, for, thought he to himself, "In the eyes of Socrates I am on the high road to the acquisition of wisdom." But the latter, perceiving him to be pleased with the praise, continued.
Soc. And what is it in which you desire to excel, Euthydemus, that you collect books?
And when Euthydemus was silent, considering what answer he should make, Socrates added: Possibly you want to be a great doctor? Why, the prescriptions[17] of the Pharmacopoeia would form a pretty large library by themselves.

[17] {suggrammata}, "medical treatises." See Aristot. "Eth." x. 9, 21.

No, indeed, not I! (answered Euthydemus).
Soc. Then do you wish to be an architect? That too implies a man of well-stored wit and judgment. [18]

[18] Or, "To be that implies a considerable store of well-packed wisdom."

I have no such ambition (he replied).
Soc. Well, do you wish to be a mathematician, like Theodorus?[19]

[19] Of Cyrene (cf. Plat. "Theaet.") taught Plato. Diog. Laert. ii. 8, 19.

Euth. No, nor yet a mathematician.

Soc. Then do you wish to be an astronomer?[20] or (as the youth signified dissent) possibly a rhapsodist?[21] (he asked), for I am told you have the entire works of Homer in your possession.[22]

[20] Cf. below, IV. vii. 4.
[21] See "Symp." iii. 6; Plat. "Ion."
[22] See Jowett, "Plato," i. 229; Grote, "Plato," i. 455.

Nay, God forbid! not I! (ejaculated the youth). Rhapsodists have a very exact acquaintance with epic poetry, I know, of course; but they are empty-pated creatures enough themselves.[23]

[23] Or, "are simply perfect in the art of reciting epic poetry, but are apt to be the veriest simpletons themselves."

At last Socrates said: Can it be, Euthydemus, that you are an aspirant to that excellence through which men become statesmen and administrators fit to rule and apt to benefit[24] the rest of the world and themselves?

[24] Or, "statesmen, and economists, and rules, and benefactors of the rest of the world and themselves."

Yes (replied he), that is the excellence I desire - beyond measure.

Upon my word (said Socrates), then you have indeed selected as the object of your ambition the noblest of virtues and the greatest of the arts, for this is the property of kings, and is entitled "royal"; but (he continued) have you considered whether it is possible to excel in these matters without being just and upright?[25]

[25] Just, {dikaios} = upright, righteous. Justice, {dikaiosune} = social uprightness = righteousness, N.T. To quote a friend: "The Greek {dikaios} combines the active dealing out of justice with the self-reflective idea of preserving justice in our conduct, which is what we mean by 'upright.'"

Euth. Certainly I have, and I say that without justice and uprightness it is impossible to be a good citizen.

No doubt (replied Socrates) you have accomplished that initial step?

Euth. Well, Socrates, I think I could hold my own against all comers as an upright man.

And have upright men (continued Socrates) their distinctive and appropriate works like those of carpenters or shoe-makers?

Euth. To be sure they have.

Soc. And just as the carpenter is able to exhibit his works and products, the righteous man should be able to expound and set forth his, should he not?

I see (replied Euthydemus) you are afraid I cannot expound the works of righteousness! Why, bless me! of course I can, and the works of unrighteousness into the bargain, since there are not a few of that sort within reach of eye and ear every day.

Shall we then (proceeded Socrates) write the letter R on this side,[26] and on that side the letter W; and then anything that appears to us to be the product of righteousness we will place to the R account, and anything which appears to be the product of wrong-doing and iniquity to the account of W?

[26] The letter R (to stand for Right, Righteous, Upright, Just). The letter W (to stand for Wrong, Unrighteous, Unjust).

By all means do so (he answered), if you think that it assists matters.

Accordingly Socrates drew the letters, as he had suggested, and continued.

Soc. Lying exists among men, does it not?

Euth. Certainly.

To which side of the account then shall we place it? (he asked).

Euth. Clearly on the side of wrong and injustice.

Soc. Deceit too is not uncommon?

Euth. By no means.

Soc. To which side shall we place deceit?

Euth. Deceit clearly on the side of wrong.

Soc. Well, and chicanery[27] or mischief of any sort?

[27] Reading {to kakourgein} (= furari, Sturz); al. {kleptein}, Stob.

Euth. That too.

Soc. And the enslavement of free-born men?[28]

[28] Or, "the kidnapping of men into slavery." {to andrapodizesthai} = the reduction of a free-born man to a state of slavery. Slavery itself ({douleia}) being regarded as the normal condition of a certain portion of the human race and not in itself immoral.

Euth. That too.

Soc. And we cannot allow any of these to lie on the R side of the account, to the side of right and justice, can we, Euthydemus?

It would be monstrous (he replied).

Soc. Very good. But supposing a man to be elected general, and he succeeds in enslaving an unjust, wicked, and hostile state, are we to say that he is doing wrong?

Euth. By no means.

Soc. Shall we not admit that he is doing what is right?

Euth. Certainly.

Soc. Again, suppose he deceives the foe while at war with them?

Euth. That would be all fair and right also.

Soc. Or steals and pillages their property? would he not be doing what is right?

Euth. Certainly; when you began I thought you were limiting the question to the case of friends.

Soc. So then everything which we set down on the side of Wrong will now have to be placed to the credit of Right?

Euth. Apparently.

Soc. Very well then, let us so place them; and please, let us make a new definition - that while it is right to do such things to a foe, it is wrong to do them to a friend, but in dealing with the latter it behoves us to be as straightforward as possible.[29]

[29] Or, "an absolutely straightforward course is necessary."

I quite assent (replied Euthydemus).

So far so good (remarked Socrates); but if a general, seeing his troops demoralised, were to invent a tale to the effect that reinforcements were coming, and by means of this false statement should revive the courage of his men, to which of the two accounts shall we place that act of fraud?[30]

[30] Cf. "Hell." IV. iii. 10; "Cyrop." I. vi. 31.

On the side of right, to my notion (he replied).

Soc. Or again, if a man chanced to have a son ill and in need of medicine, which the child refused to take, and supposing the father by an act of deceit to administer it under the guise of something nice to eat, and by service of that lie to restore the boy to health, to which account shall we set down this fraud?

Euth. In my judgment it too should be placed to the same account.

Soc. Well, supposing you have a friend in deplorably low spirits, and you are afraid he will make away with himself - accordingly you rob him of his knife or other such instrument: to which side ought we to set the theft?

Euth. That too must surely be placed to the score of right behaviour.

Soc. I understand you to say that a straightforward course is not in every case to be pursued even in dealing with friends?

Heaven forbid! (the youth exclaimed). If you will allow me, I rescind my former statement.[31]

[31] See above, I. ii. 44 ({anatithemai}).

Soc. Allow you! Of course you may - anything rather than make a false entry on our lists. . . . But there is just another point we ought not to leave uninvestigated. Let us take the case of deceiving a friend to his detriment: which is the more wrongful - to do so voluntarily or unintentionally?

Euth. Really, Socrates, I have ceased to believe in my own answers, for all my former admissions and conceptions seem to me other than I first supposed them.[32] Still, if I may hazard one more opinion, the intentional deceiver, I should say, is worse than the involuntary.

[32] Or, "all my original positions seem to me now other than I first conceived them"; or, "everything I first asserted seems now to be twisted topsy-turvy."

Soc. And is it your opinion that there is a lore and science of Right and Justice just as there is of letters and grammar?[33]

[33] {mathesis kai episteme tou dikaiou} - a doctrine and a knowledge of the Just.

Euth. That is my opinion.

Soc. And which should you say was more a man of letters[34] - he who intentionally misspells or misreads, or he who does so unconsciously?

[34] Or, "more grammatical"; "the better grammarian."

Euth. He who does so intentionally, I should say, because he can spell or read correctly whenever he chooses.

Soc. Then the voluntary misspeller may be a lettered person, but the involuntary offender is an illiterate?[35]

[35] Or, "In fact, he who sins against the lore of grammer intentionally may be a good grammarian and a man of letters, but he who does so involuntarily is illiterate and a bad grammarian?"

Euth. True, he must be. I do not see how to escape from that conclusion.

Soc. And which of the two knows what is right - he who intentionally lies and deceives, or he who lies and deceives unconsciously?[36]

[36] Or, Soc. And does he who lies and deceives with intent know what is right rather than he who

does either or both unconsciously?

Euth. Clearly he does.

Euth. The intentional and conscious liar clearly.

Soc. Well then, your statement is this: on the one hand, the man who has the knowledge of letters is more lettered than he who has no such knowledge?[37]

[37] Or, Soc. It is a fair inference, is it not, that he who has the {episteme} of grammar is more grammatical than he who has no such {episteme}?

Euth. Yes.

Soc. And he who has the {episteme} of things rightful is more righteous than he who lacks the {episteme}? See Plat. "Hipp. min."; Arist. "Eth. Eud." VI. v. 7.

Euth. Yes.

Soc. And, on the other, he who has the knowledge of what is right is more righteous than he who lacks that knowledge?

Euth. I suppose it is, but for the life of me I cannot make head or tail of my own admission.[38]

[38] Lit. "Apparently; but I appear to myself to be saying this also, heaven knows how." See Jowett, "Plato," ii. p. 416 (ed. 2).

Soc. Well (look at it like this). Suppose a man to be anxious to speak the truth, but he is never able to hold the same language about a thing for two minutes together. First he says: "The road is towards the east," and then he says, "No, it's towards the west"; or, running up a column of figures, now he makes the product this, and again he makes it that, now more, now less - what do you think of such a man?

Euth. Heaven help us! clearly he does not know what he thought he knew.

Soc. And you know the appellation given to certain people - "slavish,"[39] or, "little better than a slave?"

[39] {andropododeis}, which has the connotation of mental dulness, and a low order of intellect, cf. "boorish,' "rustic," "loutish," ("pariah," conceivably). "Slavish," "servile," with us connote moral rather than intellectual deficiency, I suppose. Hence it is impossible to preserve the humour of the Socratic argument. See Newman, op. cit. i. 107.

Euth. I do.

Soc. Is it a term suggestive of the wisdom or the ignorance of those to whom it is applied?

Euth. Clearly of their ignorance.

Soc. Ignorance, for instance, of smithying?

Euth. No, certainly not.

Soc. Then possibly ignorance of carpentering?

Euth. No, nor yet ignorance of carpentering.

Soc. Well, ignorance of shoemaking?

Euth. No, nor ignorance of any of these: rather the reverse, for the majority of those who do know just these matters are "little better than slaves."

Soc. You mean it is a title particularly to those who are ignorant of the beautiful, the good, the just? [40]

[40] Cf. Goethe's "Im Ganzen Guten Schonen resolut zu leben."

It is, in my opinion (he replied).

Soc. Then we must in every way strain every nerve to avoid the imputation of being slaves?

Euth. Nay, Socrates, by all that is holy, I did flatter myself that at any rate I was a student of philosophy, and on the right road to be taught everything essential to one who would fain make beauty and goodness his pursuit.[41] So that now you may well imagine my despair when, for all my pains expended, I cannot even answer the questions put to me about what most of all a man should know; and there is no path of progress open to me, no avenue of improvement left.

[41] {tes kalokagathias}, the virtue of the {kalos te kagathos} - nobility of soul. Cf. above, I. vi. 14.

Thereupon Socrates: Tell me, Euthydemus, have you ever been to Delphi?

Yes, certainly; twice (said he).

Soc. And did you notice an inscription somewhere on the temple: {GNOMI SEAUTON} - KNOW THYSELF?

Euth. I did.

Soc. Did you, possibly, pay no regard to the inscription? or did you give it heed and try to discover who and what you were?

I can safely say I did not (he answered). That much I made quite sure I knew, at any rate; since if I did not know even myself, what in the world did I know?

Soc. Can a man be said, do you think, to know himself who knows his own name and nothing more? or must he not rather set to work precisely like the would-be purchaser of a horse, who certainly does not think that he has got the knowledge he requires until he has discovered whether the beast is tractable or stubborn, strong or weak, quick or slow, and how it stands with the other points, serviceable or the reverse, in reference to the use and purpose of a horse? So, I say, must a man in like manner interrogate his own nature in reference to a man's requirements, and learn to know his own capacities, must he not?

Euth. Yes, so it strikes me: he who knows not his own ability knows not himself.

Soc. And this too is plain, is it not: that through self-knowledge men meet with countless blessings, and through ignorance of themselves with many evils? Because, the man who knows himself knows what is advantageous to himself; he discerns the limits of his powers, and by doing what he knows, he provides himself with what he needs and so does well; or, conversely, by holding aloof from what he knows not, he avoids mistakes and thereby mishaps. And having now a test to gauge other human beings he uses their need as a stepping-stone to provide himself with good and to avoid evil. Whereas he who does not know himself, but is mistaken as to his own capacity, is in like predicament to the rest of mankind and all human matters else; he neither knows what he wants, nor what he is doing, nor the people whom he deals with; and being all abroad in these respects, he misses what is good and becomes involved in what is ill.

Again, he that knows what he is doing through the success of his performance attains to fame and honour; his peers and co-mates are glad to make use of him, whilst his less successful neighbours, failing in their affairs, are anxious to secure his advice, his guidance, his protection;[42] they place their hopes of happiness in him, and for all these causes[43] single him out as the chief object of their affection. He, on the contrary, who knows not what he does, who chooses amiss and fails in what he puts his hands to, not only incurs loss and suffers chastisement through his blunders, but step by step loses reputation and becomes a laughing-stock, and in the end is doomed to a life of dishonour and contempt.

[42] Cf. Dante, "Tu duca, tu maestro, tu signore."
[43] Reading, {dia panta tauta}, or if {dia tauta}, translate "and therefore."

What is true of individuals is true also of communities.[44] That state which in ignorance of its power goes to war with a stronger than itself ends by being uprooted or else reduced to slavery.

[44] Or, more lit. "A law which applies, you will observe, to bodies politic."

Thereupon Euthydemus: Be assured I fully concur in your opinion; the precept KNOW THYSELF cannot be too highly valued; but what is the application? What the starting-point of self-examination? I look to you for an explanation, if you would kindly give one.[45]

[45] Or, "at what point to commence the process of self-inspection? - there is the mystery. I look to you, if you are willing, to interpret it."

Well (replied Socrates), I presume you know quite well the distinction between good and bad things: your knowledge may be relied upon so far?
Why, yes, to be sure (replied the youth); for without that much discernment I should indeed be worse than any slave.[46]

[46] Lit. "if I did not know even that."

Come then (said he), do you give me an explanation of the things so termed.
That is fortunately not hard (replied the youth). First of all, health in itself I hold to be a good, and disease in itself an evil; and in the next place the sources of either of those aforenamed, meats and drinks, and habits of life,[47] I regard as good or evil according as they contribute either to health or to disease.

[47] Or, "pursuits and occupations"; "manners and customs."

Soc. Then health and disease themselves when they prove to be soruces of any good are good, but when of any evil, evil?
And when (asked he), can health be a source of evil, or disease a source of good?
Why, bless me! often enough (replied Socrates). In the event, for instance, of some ill-starred expedition or of some disastrous voyage or other incident of the sort, of which veritably there are enough to spare - when those who owing to their health and strength take a part in the affair are lost; whilst those who were left behind - as hors de combat, on account of ill-health of other feebleness - are saved.
Euth. Yes, you are right; but you will admit that there are advantages to be got from strength and lost through weakness.
Soc. Even so; but ought we to regard those things which at one moment benefit and at another moment injure us in any strict sense good rather than evil?
Euth. No, certainly not, according to that line of argument. But wisdom,[48] Socrates, you must on your side admit, is irrefragably a good; since there is nothing which or in which a wise man would not do better than a fool.

[48] See above, III. ix. 5. Here {sophia} is not = {sophrosune}.

Soc. What say you? Have you never heard of Daedalus,[49] how he was seized by Minos on account of his wisdom, and forced to be his slave, and robbed of fatherland and freedom at one swoop? and how, while endeavouring to make his escape with his son, he caused the boy's death without effecting his own salvation, but was carried off among barbarians and again enslaved?

[49] See Ovid. "Met." viii. 159 foll., 261 foll.; Hygin. "Fab." 39, 40; Diod. Sic. iv. 79; Paus. Vii. 4. 6.

Yes, I know the old story (he answered).[50]

[50] Or, "Ah yes, of course; the tale is current."

Soc. Or have you not heard of the "woes of Palamedes,"[51] that commonest theme of song, how for his wisdom's sake Odysseus envied him and slew him?

[51] See Virg. "Aen." ii. 90; Hygin. 105; Philostr. "Her." x.

Euth. That tale also is current.

Soc. And how many others, pray, do you suppose have been seized on account of their wisdom, and despatched to the great king and at his court enslaved?[52]

[52] Cf. Herod. iii. 129.

Well, prosperity, well-being[53] (he exclaimed), must surely be a blessing, and that the most indisputable, Socrates?

[53] {to eudaimonein}, "happiness." Cf. Herod. i. 86.

It might be so (replied the philosopher) if it chanced not to be in itself a compound of other questionable blessings.

Euth. And which among the components of happiness and well-being can possibly be questionable?

None (he retorted), unless of course we are to include among these components beauty, or strength, or wealth, or reputation, or anything else of that kind?

Euth. By heaven! of course we are to include these, for what would happiness be without these?

Soc. By heaven! yes; only then we shall be including the commonest sources of mischief which befall mankind. How many are ruined by their fair faces at the hand of admireres driven to distraction[54] by the sight of beauty in its bloom! how many, tempted by their strength to essay deeds beyond their power, are involved in no small evils! how many, rendered effeminate by reason of their wealth, have been plotted against and destroyed![55] how many through fame and political power have suffered a world of woe!

[54] Cf. Plat. "Rep." vii. 517 D; "Phaedr." 249 D.
[55] e.g. Alcibiades.

Well (the youth replied) if I am not even right in praising happiness, I must confess I know not for what one ought to supplicate the gods in prayer.[56]

[56] See above for Socrates' own form of supplication.

Nay, these are matters (proceeded Socrates) which perhaps, through excessive confidence in your knowledge of them, you have failed to examine into; but since the state, which you are preparing yourself to direct, is democratically constituted,[57] of course you know what a democracy is.

[57] Or, "popularly governed."

Euth. I presume I do, decidedly.

Soc. Well, now, is it possible to know what a popular state is without knowing who the people are?

Euth. Certainly not.

Soc. And whom do you consider to be the people?

Euth. The poor citizens, I should say.

Soc. Then you know who the poor are, of course?

Euth. Of course I do.

Soc. I presume you also know who the rich are?

Euth. As certainly as I know who are the poor.

Soc. Whom do you understand by poor and rich?

Euth. By poor I mean those who have not enough to pay for their necessaries,[58] and by rich those who have more means than sufficient for all their needs.

[58] Al. "who cannot contribute their necessary quota to the taxes (according to the census)."

Soc. Have you noticed that some who possess a mere pittance not only find this sufficient, but actually succeed in getting a surplus out of it; while others do not find a large fortune large enough?

I have, most certainly; and I thank you for the reminder (replied Euthydemus). One has heard of crowned heads and despotic rulers being driven by want to commit misdeeds like the veriest paupers.

Then, if that is how matters stand (continued Socrates), we must class these same crowned heads with the commonalty; and some possessors of scant fortunes, provided they are good economists, with the wealthy?

Then Euthydemus: It is the poverty of my own wit which forces me to this admission. I bethink me it is high time to keep silence altogether; a little more, and I shall be proved to know absolutely nothing. And so he went away crestfallen, in an agony of self- contempt, persuaded that he was verily and indeed no better than a slave.

Amongst those who were reduced to a like condition by Socrates, many refused to come near him again, whom he for his part looked upon as dolts and dullards.[59] But Euthydemus had the wit to understand that, in order to become worthy of account, his best plan was to associate as much as possible with Socrates; and from that moment, save for some necessity, he never left him - in some points even imitating him in his habits and pursuits. Socrates, on his side, seeing that this was the young man's disposition, disturbed him as little as possible, but in the simplest and plainest manner initiated him into everything which he held to be needful to know or important to practise.

[59] Or, "as people of dull intelligence and sluggish temperament." Cf. Plat. "Gorg." 488 A.

III

It may be inferred that Socrates was in no hurry for those who were with him to discover capacities for speech and action or as inventive geniuses,[1] without at any rate a well-laid foundation of self-control.[2] For those who possessed such abilities without these same saving virtues would, he believed, only become worse men with greater power for mischief. His first object was to instil into those who were with him a wise spirit in their relation to the gods.[3] That such was the tenor of his conversation in dealing with men may be seen from the narratives of others who were present on some particular occasion.[4] I confine myself to a particular discussion with Euthydemus at which I was present.

[1] Or, "as speakers" (see ch. vi. below), "and men of action" (see ch. v. below), "or as masters of invention" (see ch. vii. below).

[2] Or, "but as prior to those excellences must be engrafted in them {sophrosune} (the virtues of

temperance and sanity of soul)."

[3] Lit. "His first object and endeavour was to make those who were with him {sophronas} (sound of soul) as regards the gods."

[4] Reading after Herbst, Cobet, etc., {diegountai}, or if vulg. {diegounto}, translate, "from the current accounts penned during his lifetime by the other witnesses." For {alloi} see K. Joel, op. cit. pp. 15, 23; above, "Mem." I. iv. 1.

Socrates said:[5] Tell me, Euthydemus, has it ever struck you to observe what tender pains the gods have taken to furnish man with all his needs?

[5] For the subject matter of this "teleological" chapter, see above, I. iv.; K. Joel, op. cit. Appendix, p. 547 foll. in ref. to Dummler's views.

Euth. No indeed, I cannot say that it has ever struck me.

Well (Socrates cotinued), you do not need to be reminded that, in the first place, we need light, and with light the gods supply us.

Euth. Most true, and if we had not got it we should, as far as our own eyes could help us, be like men born blind.

Soc. And then, again, seeing that we stand in need of rest and relaxation, they bestow upon us "the blessed balm of silent night."[6]

[6] {kalliston anapauterion}. The diction throughout is "poetical."

Yes (he answered), we are much beholden for that boon.

Soc. Then, forasmuch as the sun in his splendour makes manifest to us the hours of the day and bathes all things in brightness, but anon night in her darkness obliterates distinctions, have they not displayed aloft the starry orbs, which inform us of the watches of the night, whereby we can accomplish many of our needs?[7]

[7] e.g. for temple orientation see Dr. Penrose quoted by Norman Lockyer, "Nature," August 31. 1893.

It is so (he answered).

Soc. And let us not forget that the moon herself not only makes clear to us the quarters of the night, but of the month also?

Certainly (he answered).

Soc. And what of this: that whereas we need nutriment, this too the heavenly powers yield us? Out of earth's bosom they cause good to spring up[8] for our benefit; and for our benefit provide appropriate seasons to furnish us in turn not only with the many and diverse objects of need, but with the sources also of our joy and gladness?[9]

[8] Cf. Plat. "Laws," 747 D.
[9] Or, "pleasure."
Yes (he answered earerly), these things bear token truly to a love for man.[10]
[10] Cf. Plat. "Laws," 713 D; "Symp." 189 D. "These things are signs of a beneficient regard for man."

Soc. Well, and what of another priceless gift, that of water, which conspires with earth and the seasons to give both birth and increase to all things useful to us; nay, which helps to nurture our very selves, and commingling with all that feeds us, renders it more digestible, more wholesome, and more pleasant to the taste; and mark you in proportion to the abundance of our need the superabundance of its supply. What say you concerning such a boon?

Euth. In this again I see a sign of providential care.

Soc. And then the fact that the same heavenly power has provided us with fire[11] - our assistant against cold, our auxiliary in darkness, our fellow-workman in every art and every instrument which for the sake of its utility mortal man may invent or furnish himself withal. What of this, since, to put it compendiously, there is nothing serviceable to the life of man worth speaking of but owes its fabrication to fire?[12]

[11] Lit. "and then the fact that they made provision for us of even fire"; the credit of this boon, according to Hesiod, being due to Prometheus.
[12] Or, "no life-aiding appliance worthy of the name."

Euth. Yes, a transcendent instance of benevolent design.[13]

[13] Or, "Yes, that may be called an extreme instance of the divine 'philanthropy.'" Cf. Cic. "de N. D." ii. 62.

Soc. Again, consider the motions of the Sun,[14] how when he has turned him about in winter[15] he again draws nigh to us, ripening some fruits, and causing others whose time is past to dry up; how when he has fulfilled his work he comes no closer, but turns away as if in fear to scorch us to our hurt unduly; and again, when he has reached a point where if he should prolong his reatreat we should plainly be frozen to death with cold, note how he turns him about and resumes his approach, traversing that region of the heavens where he may shed his genial influence best upon us.

[14] A single MS. inserts a passage {to de kai era . . . 'Anekphraston}.
[15] i.e. as we say, "after the winter solstice."

Yes, upon my word (he answered), these occurrences bear the impress of being so ordered for the sake of man.

Soc. And then, again, it being manifest that we could not endure either scorching heat or freezing cold if they came suddenly upon us, note how gradually the sun approaches, and how gradually recedes, so that we fail to notice how we come at last to either extreme.[16]

[16] Or, "note the gradual approach and gradual recession of the sun- god, so gradual that we reach either extreme in a manner imperceptibly, and before we are aware of its severity."

For my part (he replied), the question forces itself upon my mind, whether the gods have any other occupation save only to minister to man; and I am only hindered from saying so, because the rest of animals would seem to share these benefits along with man.

Soc. Why, to be sure; and is it not plain that these animals themselves are born and bred for the sake of man? At any rate, no living creature save man derives so many of his enjoyments from sheep and goats, horses and cattle and asses, and other animals. He is more dependent, I should suppose, on these than even on plants and vegetables. At any rate, equally with these latter they serve him as means of subsistence or articles of commerce; indeed, a large portion of the human family do not use the products of the soil as food at all, but live on the milk and cheese and flesh of their flocks and herds, whilst all men everywhere tame and domesticate the more useful kinds of animals, and turn them to account as fellow-workers in war and for other purposes.

Yes, I cannot but agree with what you say (he answered), when I see that animals so much stronger than man become so subservient to his hand that he can use them as he lists.

Soc. And as we reflect on the infinite beauty and utility and the variety of nature, what are we to say of the fact that man has been endowed with sensibilities which correspond with this diversity, whereby we take our fill of every blessing;[17] or, again, this implanted faculty of reasoning, which enables us to draw inferences concerning the things which we perceive, and by aid of memory to understand how each set of things may be turned to our good, and to devise countless contrivances with a view to enjoying the good and repelling the evil; or lastly, when we consider the faculty bestowed upon us of interpretative speech, by which we are enabled to instruct one another, and to participate in all the blessings fore-named: to form societies, to establish laws, and to enter upon a civilised existence[18] - what are we to think?

[17] Or, *"Again, when we consider how many beautiful objects there are serviceable to man, and yet how unlike they are to one another, the fact that man has been endowed with senses adapted to each class of things, and so has access to a world of happiness."*
[18] *Cf. Aristot. "Pol." III. ix. 5.*

Euth. Yes, Socrates, decidely it would appear that the gods do manifest a great regard, nay, a tender care, towards mankind.

Soc. Well, and what do you make of the fact that where we are powerless to take advantageous forethought for our future, at this stage they themselves lend us their co-operation, imparting to the inquirer through divination knowledge of events about to happen, and instructing him by what means they may best be turned to good account?

Euth. Ay, and you, Socrates, they would seem to treat in a more friendly manner still than the rest of men, if, without waiting even to be inquired of by you, they show you by signs beforehand what you must, and what you must not do.[19]

[19] *See above, I. iv. 14, for a parallel to the train of thought on the part of Aristodemus "the little," and of Euthydemus; and for Socrates' {daimonion}, see above; Grote, "Plato," i. 400.*

Soc. Yes, and you will discover for youself the truth of what I say, if, without waiting to behold the outward and visible forms[20] of the gods themselves, you will be content to behold their works; and with these before you, to worship and honour the Divine authors of them.[21] I would have you reflect that the very gods themselves suggest this teaching.[22] Not one of these but gives us freely of his blessings; yet they do not step from behind their veil in order to grant one single boon.[23] And pre-eminently He who orders and holds together the universe,[24] in which are all things beautiful and good; [25] who fashions and refashions it to never-ending use unworn, keeping it free from sickness or decay, [26] so that swifter than thought it ministers to his will unerringly - this God is seen to perform the mightiest operations, but in the actual administration of the same abides himself invisible to mortal ken. Reflect further, this Sun above our heads, so visible to all - as we suppose - will not suffer man to regard him too narrowly, but should any essay to watch him with a shameless stare he will snatch away their power of vision. And if the gods themselves are thus unseen, so too shall you find their ministers to be hidden also; from the height of heaven above the thunderbolt is plainly hurled, and triumphs over all that it encounters, yet it is all-invisible, no eye may detect its coming or its going at the moment of its swoop. The winds also are themselves unseen, though their works are manifest, and through their approach we are aware of them. And let us not forget, the soul of man himself, which if aught else human shares in the divine - however manifestly enthroned within our bosom, is as wholly as the rest hidden from our gaze. These things you should lay to mind, and not despise the invisible ones, but learn to recognise their power, as revealed in outward things, and to know the divine influence.[27]

[20] Cf. Cic. "de N. D." I. xii. 31; Lactantius, "de Ira," xi. 13.

[21] See L. Dindorf ad loc. (ed. Ox. 1862), {theous}; G. Sauppe, vol. iii. "An. crit." p. xxix; R. Kuhner; C. Schenkl.

[22] i.e. "that man must walk by faith." For {upodeiknunai} cf. "Econ." xii. 18.

[23] Schneid. cf. Plat. "Crat." 396.

[24] Or, "the co-ordinator and container of the universe."

[25] Or, "in whom all beauty and goodness is."

[26] Cf. "Cyrop." VIII. vii. 22; above, I. iv. 13.

[27] {to daimonion}, the divinity.

Nay, Socrates (replied Euthydemus), there is no danger I shall turn a deaf ear to the divine influence even a little; of that I am not afraid, but I am out of heart to think that no soul of man may ever requite the kindness of the gods with fitting gratitude.

Be not out of heart because of that (he said); you know what answer the god at Delphi makes to each one who comes asking "how shall I return thanks to heaven?" - "According to the law and custom of your city"; and this, I presume, is law and custom everywhere that a man should please the gods with offerings according to the ability which is in him.[28] How then should a man honour the gods with more beautiful or holier honour than by doing what they bid him? but he must in no wise slacken or fall short of his ability, for when a man so does, it is manifest, I presume, that at the moment he is not honouring the gods. You must then honour the gods, not with shortcoming but according to your ability; and having so done, be of good cheer and hope to receive the greatest blessings. For where else should a man of sober sense look to receive great blessings if not from those who are able to help him most, and how else should he hope to obtain them save by seeking to please his helper, and how may he hope to please his helper better than by yielding him the amplest obedience?

[28] Or, "and that law, I presume, is universal which says, Let a man," etc.; and for the maxim see above; "Anab." III. ii. 9.

By such words - and conduct corresponding to his words - did Socrates mould and fashion the hearts of his companions, making them at once more devout and more virtuous.[29]

[29] Or, "sounder of soul and more temperate as well as more pious."

IV

But indeed[1] with respect to justice and uprightness he not only made no secret of the opinion he held, but gave practical demonstration of it, both in private by his law-abiding and helpful behaviour to all,[2] and in public by obeying the magistrates in all that the laws enjoined, whether in the life of the city or in military service, so that he was a pattern of loyalty to the rest of the world, and on three several occasions in particular: first, when as president (Epistates) of the assembly he would not suffer the sovereign people to take an unconstitutional vote,[3] but ventured, on the side of the laws, to resist a current of popular feeling strong enough, I think, to have daunted any other man. Again, when the Thirty tried to lay some injunction on him contrary to the laws, he refused to obey, as for instance when they forbade his conversing with the young;[4] or again, when they ordered him and certain other citizens to arrest a man to be put to death,[5] he stood out single-handed on the ground that the injunctions laid upon him were contrary to the laws. And lastly, when he appeared as defendant in the suit instituted by Meletus,[6] notwithstanding that it was customary for litigants in the law courts to humour the judges in the conduct of their arguments by flattery and supplications contrary to the laws,[7] notwithstanding also that defendants owed their acquittal by the court to the employment of such methods, he refused to do a single thing however habitual in a court of law which was not strictly legal; and though by only a slight deflection from the strict path he might easily have been acquitted by his judges,[8] he preferred to abide by the laws and die rather than transgress them and live.

[1] *L. Dindorf suspects [SS. 1-6, {'Alla men . . . pollakis}], ed. Lips. 1872. See also Praef. to Ox. ed. p. viii.*

[2] *Or, "by his conduct to all, which was not merely innocent in the eye of law and custom but positively helpful."*

[3] *See above, I. i. 18; "Hell." I. vii. 14, 15; Grote, "H. G." viii. 272.*

[4] *See above, I. ii. 35.*

[5] *Leon of Salamis. See "Hell." II. iii. 39; Plat. "Apol." 32 C; Andoc. "de Myst." 46.*

[6] *See above, I. i. 1; Plat. "Apol." 19 C.*

[7] *Kuhner cf. Quintil. VI. i. 7: "Athenis affectus movere etiam per praeconem prohibatur orator"; "Apol." 4; Plat. "Apol." 38 D, E.*

[8] *See Grote, "H. G." viii. p. 663 foll.*

These views he frequently maintained in conversation, now with one and now with another, and one particular discussion with Hippias of Elis[9] on the topic of justice and uprightness has come to my knowledge.[10]

[9] *For this famous person see Cob. "Pros. Xen." s.n.; Plat. "Hipp. maj." 148; Quint. xii. 11, 21; Grote, "H. G." viii. 524.*

[10] *Or, "I can personally vouch for."*

Hippias had just arrived at Athens after a long absence, and chanced to be present when Socrates was telling some listeners how astonishing it was that if a man wanted to get another taught to be a shoemaker or carpenter or coppersmith or horseman, he would have no doubt where to send him for the purpose: "People say,"[11] he added, "that if a man wants to get his horse or his ox taught in the right way,[12] the world is full of instructors; but if he would learn himself, or have his son or his slave taught in the way of right, he cannot tell where to find such instruction."

[11] *L. Dindorf, after Ruhnken and Valckenar, omits this sentence {phasi de tines . . . didaxonton}. See Kuhner ad loc. For the sentiment see Plat. "Apol." 20 A.*

[12] *Cf. "Cyrop." II. ii. 26; VIII. iii. 38; also "Horsem." iii. 5; "Hunting," vii. 4.*

Hippias, catching the words, exclaimed in a bantering tone: What! still repeating the same old talk, [13] Socrates, which I used to hear from you long ago?

[13] *This tale is repeated by Dio Chrys. "Or." III. i. 109. Cf. Plat. "Gorg." 490 E.*

Yes (answered Socrates), and what is still more strange, Hippias, it is not only the same old talk but about the same old subjects. Now you, I daresay, through versatility of knowledge,[14] never say the same thing twice over on the same subject?

[14] *Or, "such is the breadth of your learning," {polumathes}. Cf. Plat. "Hipp. maj."*

To be sure (he answered), my endeavour is to say something new on all occasions.

What (he asked) about things which you know, as for instance in a case of spelling, if any one asks you, "How many letters in Socrates, and what is their order?"[15] I suppose you try to run off one string of letters to-day and to-morrow another? or to a question of arithmetic, "Does twice five make ten?" your answer to-day will differ from that of yesterday?

[15] Cf. "Econ." viii. 14; Plat. "Alc." i. 113 A.

Hipp. No; on these topics, Socrates, I do as you do and repeat myself. However, to revert to justice (and uprightness),[16] I flatter myself I can at present furnish you with some remarks which neither you nor any one else will be able to controvert.

[16] Or, "on the topic of the just I have something to say at present which," etc.

By Hera![17] (he exclaimed), what a blessing to have discovered![18] Now we shall have no more divisions of opinion on points of right and wrong; judges will vote unanimously; citizens will cease wrangling; there will be no more litigation, no more party faction, states will reconcile their differences, and wars are ended. For my part I do not know how I can tear myself away from you, until I have heard from your own lips all about the grand discovery you have made.

[17] See above, I. v. 5.
[18] Or, "what a panacea are you the inventor of"; lit. "By Hera, you have indeed discovered a mighty blessing, if juries are to cease recording their verdicts 'aye' and 'no'; if citizens are to cease their wranglings on points of justice, their litigations, and their party strifes; if states are to cease differing on matters of right and wrong and appealing to the arbitrament of war."

You shall hear all in good time (Hippias answered), but not until you make a plain statement of your own belief. What is justice? We have had enough of your ridiculing all the rest of the world, questioning and cross-examining first one and then the other, but never a bit will you render an account to any one yourself or state a plain opinion upon a single topic.[19]

[19] See Plat. "Gorg." 465 A.

What, Hippias (Socrates retorted), have you not observed that I am in a chronic condition of proclaiming what I regard as just and upright?
Hipp. And pray what is this theory[20] of yours on the subject? Let us have it in words.

[20] {o logos}.

Soc. If I fail to proclaim it in words, at any rate I do so in deed and in fact. Or do you not think that a fact is worth more as evidence than a word?[21]

[21] Or, "is of greater evidential value," "ubi res adsunt, quid opus est verbis?"

Worth far more, I should say (Hippias answered), for many a man with justice and right on his lips commits injustice and wrong, but no doer of right ever was a misdoer or could possibly be.
Soc. I ask then, have you ever heard or seen or otherwise perceived me bearing false witness or lodging malicious information, or stirring up strife among friends or political dissension in the city, or committing any other unjust and wrongful act?
No, I cannot say that I have (he answered).
Soc. And do you not regard it as right and just to abstain from wrong?[22]

[22] Or, "is not abstinence from wrongdoing synonymous with righteous behaviour?"

Hipp. Now you are caught, Socrates, plainly trying to escape from a plain statement. When asked what you believe justice to be, you keep telling us not what the just man does, but what he does not do.

Why, I thought for my part (answered Socrates) that the refusal to do wrong and injustice was a sufficient warrent in itself of righteousness and justice, but if you do not agree, see if this pleases you better: I assert that what is "lawful" is "just and righteous."

Do you mean to assert (he asked) that lawful and just are synonymous terms?

Soc. I do.

I ask (Hippias added), for I do not perceive what you mean by lawful, nor what you mean by just.[23]

[23] Lit. "what sort of lawful or what sort of just is spoken of."

Soc. You understand what is meant by laws of a city or state?

Yes (he answered).

Soc. What do you take them to be?

Hipp. The several enactments drawn up by the citizens or members of a state in agreement as to what things should be done or left undone.

Then I presume (Socrates continued) that a member of a state who regulates his life in accordance with these enactments will be law- abiding, while the transgressor of the same will be law-less?

Certainly (he answered).

Soc. And I presume the law-loving citizen will do what is just and right, while the lawless man will do what is unjust and wrong?

Hipp. Certainly.

Soc. And I presume that he who does what is just is just, and he who does what is unjust is unjust?

Hipp. Of course.

Soc. It would appear, then, that the law-loving man is just, and the lawless unjust?

Then Hippias: Well, but laws, Socrates, how should any one regard as a serious matter either the laws themselves, or obedience to them, which laws the very people who made them are perpetually rejecting and altering?

Which is also true of war (Socrates replied); cities are perpetually undertaking war and then making peace again.

Most true (he answered).

Soc. If so, what is the difference between depreciating obedience to law because laws will be repealed, and depreciating good discipline in war because peace will one day be made? But perhaps you object to enthusiasm displayed in defence of one's home and fatherland in war?

No, indeed I do not! I heartily approve of it (he answered).

Soc. Then have you laid to heart the lesson taught by Lycurgus to the Lacedaemonians,[24] and do you understand that if he succeeded in giving Sparta a distinction above other states, it was only by instilling into her, beyond all else, a spirit of obedience to the laws? And among magistrates and rulers in the different states, you would scarcely refuse the palm of superiority to those who best contribute to make their fellow-citizens obedient to the laws? And you would admit that any particular state in which obedience to the laws is the paramount distinction of the citizens flourishes most in peace time, and in time of war is irresistible? But, indeed, of all the blessings which a state may enjoy, none stands higher than the blessing of unanimity. "Concord among citizens" - that is the constant theme of exhortation emphasised by the councils of elders[25] and by the choice spirits of the community;[26] at all times and everywhere through the length and breadth of all Hellas it is an established law that the citizens be bound together by an oath of concord;[27] everywhere they do actually swear this oath; not of course as implying that citizens shall all vote for the same choruses, or give their plaudits to the same flute-players, or choose the same poets, or limit themselves to the same pleasures, but simply that they shall pay obedience to the laws, since in the end that state will prove most powerful and most prosperous in which the citizens abide by these; but without concord neither can a state be well administered nor a household well organised.

[24] Cf. "Pol. Lac." viii. See Newman, op. cit. i. 396.
[25] Lit. "the Gerousiai." {S} or {X S} uses the Spartan phraseology.
[26] Lit. "the best men." {S} or {X S} speaks as an "aristocrat."
[27] Cf. "Hell." II. iv. 43; Lys. xxv. 21 foll.; Schneid. cf. Lycurg. "u Leocr." 189.

And if we turn to private life, what better protection can a man have than obedience to the laws? This shall be his safeguard against penalties, his guarantee of honours at the hands of the community; it shall be a clue to thread his way through the mazes of the law courts unbewildered, secure against defeat, assured of victory.[28] It is to him, the law-loving citizen, that men will turn in confidence when seeking a guardian of the most sacred deposits, be it of money or be it their sons or daughters. He, in the eyes of the state collectively, is trustworthy - he and no other; who alone may be depended on to render to all alike their dues - to parents and kinsmen and servants, to friends and fellow-citizens and foreigners. This is he whom the enemy will soonest trust to arrange an armistice, or a truce, or a treaty of peace. They would like to become the allies of this man, and to fight on his side. This is he to whom the allies[29] of his country will most confidently entrust the command of their forces, or of a garrison, or their states themselves. This, again, is he who may be counted on to recompense kindness with gratitude, and who, therefore, is more sure of kindly treatment than another whose sense of gratitude is fuller.[30] The most desirable among friends, the enemy of all others to be avoided, clearly he is not the person whom a foreign state would choose to go to war with; encompassed by a host of friends and exempt from foes, his very character has a charm to compel friendship and alliance, and before him hatred and hostility melt away.

[28] Or, "ignorant of hostile, assured of favourable verdict."
[29] Lit. "the Allies," e.g. of Sparta or of Athens, etc.
[30] Lit. "From whom may the doer of a deed of kindness more confidently expect the recompense of gratitude than from your lover of the law? and whom would one select as the recipient of kindness rather than a man susceptible of gratitude?"

And now, Hippias, I have done my part; that is my proof and demonstration that the "lawful" and "law-observant" are synonymous with the "upright" and the "just"; do you, if you hold a contrary view, instruct us.[31]

[31] For the style of this enconium (of the {nomimos}) cf. "Ages." i. 36; and for the "Socratic" reverence for law cf. Plat. "Crito."

Then Hippias: Nay, upon my soul, Socrates, I am not aware of holding any contrary opinion to what you have uttered on the theme of justice.[32]

[32] Lit. "the just and upright," {tou dikaiou}.

Soc. But now, are you aware, Hippias, of certain unwritten laws?[33]

[33] See Soph. "Antig." "Oed. T." 865, and Prof. Jebb ad loc.; Dem. "de Cor." 317, 23; Aristot. "Rhet." I. xiii.

Yes (he answered), those held in every part of the world, and in the same sense.

Can you then assert (asked Socrates) of these unwritten laws that men made them?

Nay, how (he answered) should that be, for how could they all have come together from the ends of the earth? and even if they had so done, men are not all of one speech?[34]

[34] Or, "there would be difficulty of understanding each other, and a babel of tongues."

Soc. Whom then do you believe to have been the makers of these laws.

Hipp. For my part, I think that the gods must have made these laws for men, and I take it as proof that first and foremost it is a law and custom everywhere to worship and reverence the gods.

Soc. And, I presume, to honour parents is also customary everywhere?

Yes, that too (he answered).

Soc. And, I presume, also the prohibition of intermarriage between parents and children?

Hipp. No; at that point I stop, Socrates. That does not seem to me to be a law of God.

Now, why? (he asked).

Because I perceive it is not infrequently transgressed (he answered).[35]

[35] Or, "as I perceive, it is not of universal application, some transgress it."

Soc. Well, but there are a good many other things which people do contrary to law; only the penalty, I take it, affixed to the transgression of the divine code is certain; there is no escape for the offender after the manner in which a man may transgress the laws of man with impunity, slipping through the fingers of justice by stealth, or avoiding it by violence.

Hipp. And what is the inevitable penalty paid by those who, being related as parents and children, intermingle in marriage?

Soc. The greatest of all penalties; for what worse calamity can human beings suffer in the production of offspring than to misbeget?[36]

[36] Or, "in the propagation of the species than to produce misbegotten children."

Hipp. But how or why should they breed them ill where nothing hinders them, being of a good stock themselves and producing from stock as good?

Soc. Because, forsooth, in order to produce good children, it is not simply necessary that the parents should be good and of a good stock, but that both should be equally in the prime and vigour of their bodies.[37] Do you suppose that the seed of those who are at their prime is like theirs who either have not yet reached their prime, or whose prime has passed?

[37] Cf. Plat. "Laws," viii. 839 A; Herbst, etc., cf. Grotius, "de Jure," ii. 5, xii. 4.

Hipp. No, it is reasonable to expect that the seed will differ.

Soc. And for the better - which?

Hipp. Theirs clearly who are at their prime.

Soc. It would seem that the seed of those who are not yet in their prime or have passed their prime is not good?

Hipp. It seems most improbable it should be.

Soc. Then the right way to produce children is not that way?

Hipp. No, that is not the right way.

Soc. Then children who are so produced are produced not as they ought to be?

Hipp. So it appears to me.

What offspring then (he asked) will be ill produced, ill begotten, and ill born, if not these?

I subscribe to that opinion also (replied Hippias).

Soc. Well, it is a custom universally respected, is it not, to return good for good, and kindness with kindness?

Hipp. Yes, a custom, but one which again is apt to be transgressed.

Soc. Then he that so transgresses it pays penalty in finding himself isolated; bereft of friends who are good, and driven to seek after those who love him not. Or is it not so that he who does me kindness in my intercourse with him is my good friend, but if I requite not this kindness to my benefactor, I am hated by him for my ingratitude, and yet I must needs pursue after him and cling to him because of the great gain to me of his society?

Hipp. Yes, Socrates. In all these cases, I admit, there is an implication of divine authority;[38] that a law should in itself be loaded with the penalty of its transgression does suggest to my mind a higher than human type of legistlator.

[38] Lit. "Yes, upon my word, Socrates, all these cases look very like (would seem to point to) the gods."

Soc. And in your opinion, Hippias, is the legislation of the gods just and righteous, or the reverse of what is just and righteous?

Hipp. Not the reverse of what is just and righteous, Socrates, God forbid! for scarcely could any other legislate aright, of not God himself.

Soc. It would seem then, Hippias, the gods themselves are well pleased that "the lawful" and "the just" should be synonymous?[39]

[39] Or, "it is well pleasing also to the gods that what is lawful is just and what is just is lawful."

By such language and by such conduct, through example and precept alike, he helped to make those who approached him more upright and more just.

V

And now I propose to show in what way he made those who were with him more vigorous in action.[1] In the first place, as befitted one whose creed was that a basis of self-command is indispensable to any noble performance, he manifested himself to his companions as one who had pre-eminently disciplined himself;[2] and in the next place by conversation and discussion he encouraged them to a like self-restraint beyond all others.[3] Thus it was that he continued ever mindful himself, and was continually reminding all whom he encountered, of matters conducive to virtue; as the following discussion with Euthydemus, which has come to my knowledge,[4] will serve to illustrate - the topic of the discussion being self-command.

[1] Lit. "more practical," i.e. more energetic and effective.
[2] "If any one might claim to be a prince of ascetics, it was Socrates; such was the ineffaceable impression left on the minds of his associates."
[3] Or, "he stimulated in these same companions a spirit of self-restraint beyond all else."
[4] Or, "which I can vouch for."

Tell me, Euthydemus (he began), do you believe freedom to be a noble and magnificent acquisition, whether for a man or for a state?

I cannot conceive a nobler or more magnificent (he answered).

Soc. Then do you believe him to be a free man who is ruled by the pleasures of the body, and thereby cannot perform what is best?

Certainly not (he answered).

Soc. No! for possibly to perform what is best appears to you to savour of freedom? And, again, to have some one over you who will prevent you doing the like seems a loss of freedom?

Most decidedly (he answered).

Soc. It would seem you are decidedly of opinion that the incontinent are the reverse of free?[5]

[5] Or, "incontinency is illiberal."

Euth. Upon my word, I much suspect so.

Soc. And does it appear to you that the incontinent man is merely hindered from doing what is noblest, or that further he is impelled to do what is most shameful?

Euth. I think he is as much driven to the one as he is hindered from the other.

Soc. And what sort of lords and masters are those, think you, who at once put a stop to what is best and enforce what is worst?

Euth. Goodness knows, they must be the very worst of masters.

Soc. And what sort of slavery do you take to be the worst?

I should say (he answered) slavery to the worst masters.

It would seem then (pursued Socrates) that the incontinent man is bound over to the worst sort of slavery, would it not?

So it appears to be (the other answered).

Soc. And does it not appear to you that this same beldame incontinence shuts out wisdom, which is the best of all things,[6] from mankind, and plunges them into the opposite? Does it not appear to you that she hinders men from attending to things which will be of use and benefit, and from learning to understand them; that she does so by dragging them away to things which are pleasant; and often though they are well aware of the good and of the evil, she amazes and confounds[7] their wits and makes them choose the worse in place of the better?

[6] "Wisdom, the greatest good which men can possess."
[7] Schneid. cf. Plat. "Protag." 355 A; and "Symp." iv. 23.

Yes, so it comes to pass (he answered).

Soc. And[8] soundness of soul, the spirit of temperate modesty? Who has less claim to this than the incontinent man? The works of the temperate spirit and the works of incontinency are, I take it, diametrically opposed?

[8] "And if this be so concerning wisdom, {sophia}, what of {sophrasune}, soundness of soul - sobriety?"

That too, I admit (he answered).

Soc. If this then be so concerning these virtues,[9] what with regard to carefulness and devotion to all that ought to occupy us? Can anything more seriously militate against these than this same incontinence?

[9] Or add, "If this be so concerning not wisdom only, but concerning temperance and soundness of soul, what," etc.

Nothing that I can think of (he replied).

Soc. And can worse befall a man, think you? Can he be subjected to a more baleful influence than that which induces him to choose what is hurtful in place of what is helpful; which cajoles him to devote himself to the evil and to neglect the good; which forces him, will he nill he, to do what every man in his sober senses would shrink from and avoid?

I can imagine nothing worse (he replied).

Soc. Self-control, it is reasonable to suppose, will be the cause of opposite effects upon mankind to those of its own opposite, the want of self-control?

Euth. It is to be supposed so.

Soc. And this, which is the source of opposite effects to the very worst, will be the very best of things?

Euth. That is the natural inference.

Soc. It looks, does it not, Euthydemus, as if self-control were the best thing a man could have?

It does indeed, Socrates (he answered).

Soc. But now, Euthydemus, has it ever occurred to you to note one fact?

What fact? (he asked).

Soc. That, after all, incontinency is powerless to bring us to that realm of sweetness which some look upon[10] as her peculiar province; it is not incontinency but self-control alone which has the passport to highest pleasures.

[10] Or, "which we are apt to think of as."

In what way? (he asked). How so?

Why, this way (Socrates answered): since incontinency will not suffer us to resist hunger and thirst, or to hold out against sexual appetite, or want of sleep (which abstinences are the only channels to true pleasure in eating and drinking, to the joys of love, to sweet repose and blissful slumber won by those who will patiently abide and endure till each particular happiness is at the flood)[11] - it comes to this: by incontinency we are cut off from the full fruition of the more obvious and constantly recurring pleasures.[12] To self-control, which alone enables us to endure the pains aforesaid, alone belongs the power to give us any pleasure worth remembering in these common cases.

[11] Or, "at its season." Lit. "is as sweet as possible."
[12] Or, "from tasting to any extent worth speaking of the most necessary and all-pervading sources of happiness."

You speak the words of truth[13] (he answered).

[13] Lit. "What you say is absolutely and entirely true" (the "vraie verite" of the matter).

Soc. Furthermore,[14] if there be any joy in learning aught "beautiful and good," or in patient application to such rules as may enable a man to manage his body aright, or to administer his household well, or to prove himself useful to his friends and to the state, or to dominate his enemies - which things are the sources not only of advantage but of deepest satisfaction[15] - to the continent and self-controlled it is given to reap the fruits of them in their performance. It is the incontinent who have neither part nor lot in any one of them. Since we must be right in asserting that he is least concerned with such things who has least ability to do them, being tied down to take an interest in the pleasure which is nearest to hand.

[14] Or, "But indeed, if there be joy in the pursuit of any noble study or of such accomplishments as shall enable," etc.

[15] Or, "of the highest pleasures."

Euthydemus replied: Socrates, you would say, it seems to me, that a man who is mastered by the pleasures of the body has no concern at all with virtue.

And what is the distinction, Euthydemus (he asked), between a man devoid of self-control and the dullest of brute beasts? A man who foregoes all height of aim, who gives up searching for the best and strives only to gratify his sense of pleasure,[16] is he better than the silliest of cattle?[17] . . . But to the self-controlled alone is it given to discover the hid treasures. These, by word and by deed, they will pick out and make selection of them according to their kinds, choosing deliberately the good and holding aloof from the evil.[18] Thus (he added) it is that a man reaches the zenith, as it were, of goodness and happiness, thus it is that he becomes most capable of reasoning and discussion.[19] The very name discussion ({dialegesthai}) is got from people coming together and deliberating in common by picking out and selecting things ({dialegein}) according to their kinds.[20] A man then is bound to prepare himself as much as possible for this business, and to pursue it beyond all else with earnest resolution; for this is the right road to excellence, this will make a man fittest to lead his fellows and be a master in debate.[21]

[16] Or, "and seeks by hook and by crook to do what is pleasantest."
[17] i.e. he becomes an animal "feeding a blind life within the brain."
[18] Or, "selecting the ore and repudiating the dross." Kuhner cf. Plat. "Laws," v. 735 B.
[19] Or, "draws nearer to happiness and perfection, and is most capable of truth-disclosing conversation." Cf. Plat. "Apol." 41: "What would not a man give, O judges, to be able to examine the leaders of the great Trojan expedition, or Odysseus, or Sisyphus, or numberless others, men and women too! What infinite delight would there be in conversing with them and asking them questions!" (Jowett).
[20] For {dialegein kata gene} = {dialegesthai}, cf. Grote, "H. G." viii. 590.
[21] Cf. Plat. "Rep." 534 D; "Phaedr." 252 E; "Crat." 390 C; "Statesm." 286 D foll.

VI

At this point I will endeavour to explain in what way Socrates fostered this greater "dialectic" capacity among his intimates.[1] He held firmly to the opinion that if a man knew what each reality was, he would be able to explain this knowledge to others; but, failing the possession of that knowledge, it did not surprise him that men should stumble themselves and cause others to stumble also.[2] It was for this reason that he never ceased inquiring with those who were with him into the true nature of things that are.[3] It would be a long business certainly to go through in detail all the definitions at which he arrived; I will therefore content myself with such examples as will serve to show his method of procedure. As a first instance I will take the question of piety. The mode of investigation may be fairly represented as follows.

[1] Lit. "essayed to make those who were with him more potent in dialectic."
[2] Or, "Socrates believed that any one who knew the nature of anything would be able to let others into his secret; but, failing that knowledge, he thought the best of men would be but blind leaders of the blind, stumbling themselves and causing others to stumble also."
[3] Or add, "'What is this among things? and what is its definition?' - such was the ever-recurrent question for which he sought an answer."

Tell me (said he), Euthydemus, what sort of thing you take piety to be?
Something most fair and excellent, no doubt (the other answered).[4]

[4] Or, "A supreme excellence, no doubt."

Soc. And can you tell me what sort of person the pious man is?[5]

[5] Or, "can you give me a definition of the pious man?"; "tell me who and what the pious man is."

I should say (he answered) he is a man who honours the gods.
Soc. And is it allowable to honour the gods in any mode or fashion one likes?
Euth. No; there are laws in accordance with which one must do that.
Soc. Then he who knows these laws will know how he must honour the gods?
I think so (he answered).
Soc. And he who knows how he must honour the gods conceives that he ought not to do so except in the manner which accords with his knowledge?[6] Is it not so?

[6] i.e. "his practice must square with his knowledge and be the outward expression of his belief?"

Euth. That is so.[7]

[7] "That is so; you rightly describe his frame of mind and persuasion."

Soc. And does any man honour the gods otherwise than he thinks he ought?[8]

[8] "As he should and must." See K. Joel, op. cit. p. 322 foll.

I think not (he answered).
Soc. It comes to this then: he who knows what the law requires in reference to the gods will honour the gods in the lawful way?[9]

[9] Or, "he who knows what is lawful with regard to Heaven pays honour to Heaven lawfully."

Euth. Certainly.
Soc. But now, he who honours lawfully honours as he ought?[10]

[10] "As he should and must."

Euth. I see no alternative.
Soc. And he who honours as he ought is a pious man?
Euth. Certainly.
Soc. It would appear that he who knows what the law requires with respect to the gods will correctly be defined as a pious man, and that is our definition?
So it appears to me, at any rate (he replied).[11]

[11] "I accept it at any rate as mine." N.B. - in reference to this definition of Piety, the question is never raised {poion ti esti nomos}; nor yet {poioi tines eisin oi theoi}; but clearly there is a growth in {ta nomima}. Cf. the conversation recorded in St. John iv. 7 foll., and the words (verse 23) {pneuma o Theos kai tous proskunountas auton en pneumati kai aletheia dei proskunein}, which the philosopher Socrates would perhaps readily have assented to.

Soc. But now, with regard to human beings; is it allowable to deal with men in any way one pleases?

[12]

[12] Or, "may a man deal with his fellow-men arbitrarily according to his fancy?" See above, II. vii. 8.

Euth. No; with regard to men also, he will be a law-observing man[13] who knows what things are lawful as concerning men, in accordance with which our dealings with one another must be conducted. [14]

[13] Or, "he is a man full of the law (lawful) and law-abiding who knows," etc.
[14] Reading {kath' a dei pros allelous khresthai}, subaud. {allelois}, or if vulg. {kath' a dei pos allelois khresthai}, translate "must be specifically conducted."

Soc. Then those who deal with one another in this way, deal with each other as they ought?[15]

[15] "As they should and must."

Obviously (he answered).
Soc. And they who deal with one another as they ought, deal well and nobly - is it not so?
Certainly (he answered).
Soc. And they who deal well and nobly by mankind are well-doers in respect of human affairs?
That would seem to follow (he replied).
Soc. I presume that those who obey the laws do what is just and right?
Without a doubt, (he answered).
Soc. And by things right and just you know what sort of things are meant?
What the laws ordain (he answered).
Soc. It would seem to follow that they who do what the laws ordain both do what is right and just and what they ought?[16]

[16] "What they should and must."

Euth. I see no alternative.
Soc. But then, he who does what is just and right is upright and just?[17]

[17] This proposition, as Kuhner argues (ad loc.), is important as being the middle term of the double syllogism (A and B) -

A. Those who do what the law demands concerning men do what is just and right.
Those who do what is just and right are righteous and just.
Ergo - Those who do what the law demands concerning men are righteous and just.
B. Those who know what is just and right ought (and are bound, cf. above, III. ix. 4) to do also what is just and right.
Those who do what is just and right are righteous and just.
Ergo - Righteous and Just ({dikaioi}) may be defined as "Those who know what the law demands (aliter things right and just) concerning men."
I should say so myself (he answered).
Soc. And should you say that any one obeys the laws without knowing what the laws ordain?
I should not (he answered).
Soc. And do you suppose that any one who knows what things he ought to do supposes that he ought

not to do them?[18]

[18] Or, "and no one who knows what he must and should do imagines that he must and should not do it?"

No, I suppose not (he answered).
Soc. And do you know of anybody doing other than what he feels bound to do?[19]

[19] Or, "and nobody that you know of does the contrary of what he thinks he should do?"

No, I do not (he answered).
Soc. It would seem that he who knows what things are lawful[20] as concerning men does the things that are just and right?

[20] Or, "of lawful obligation."

Without a doubt (he answered).
Soc. But then, he who does what is just and right is upright and just?[21]

[21] N.B. - In reference to this definition of justice, see K. Joel, op. cit. p. 323 foll., "Das ist eine Karrikatur des Sokratischen Dialogs."

Who else, if not? (he replied).
Soc. It would seem, then, we shall have got to a right definition if we name as just and upright those who know the things which are lawful as concerning men?
That is my opinion (he answered).
Soc. And what shall we say that wisdom is? Tell me, does it seem to you that the wise are wise in what they know,[22] or are there any who are wise in what they know not?

[22] Or, "in that of which they have the knowledge ({episteme})."

Euth. Clearly they are wise in what they know;[23] for how could a man have wisdom in that which he does not know?

[23] Or, "their wisdom is confined to that of which they have the {episteme}. How could a man be wise in what he lacks the knowledge of?"

Soc. In fact, then, the wise are wise in knowledge?
Euth. Why, in what else should a man be wise save only in knowledge?
Soc. And is wisdom anything else than that by which a man is wise, think you?
Euth. No; that, and that only, I think.
Soc. It would seem to follow that knowledge and wisdom are the same?
Euth. So it appears to me.
Soc. May I ask, does it seem to you possible for a man to know all the things that are?
Euth. No, indeed! not the hundredth part of them, I should say.
Soc. Then it would seem that it is impossible for a man to be all- wise?
Quite impossible (he answered).
Soc. It would seem the wisdom of each is limited to his knowledge; each is wise only in what he knows?

Euth. That is my opinion.[24]

Soc. Well! come now, Euthydemus, as concerning the good: ought we to search for the good in this way?
What way? (he asked).
Soc. Does it seem to you that the same thing is equally advantageous to all?
No, I should say not (he answered).
Soc. You would say that a thing which is beneficial to one is sometimes hurtful to another?
Decidedly (he replied).
Soc. And is there anything else good except that which is beneficial, should you say?[25]

[25] Or reading (1) {allo d' an ti phaies e agathon einai to ophelimon}; or else (2) {allo d' an ti phaies agathon einai to ophelimon}; (in which case {alloti} = {allo ti e};) translate (1) "and what is beneficial is good (or a good), should you not say?" lit. "could you say that the beneficial is anything else than good (or a good)?" or else (2) "and what is beneficial is good (or a good)? or is it anything else?"

Nothing else (he answered).
Soc. It would seem to follow that the beneficial is good relatively to him to whom it is beneficial?
That is how it appears to me (he answered).
Soc. And the beautiful: can we speak of a thing as beautiful in any other way than relatively? or can you name any beautiful thing, body, vessel, or whatever it be, which you know of as universally beautiful?[26]

[26] i.e. "beautiful in all relations into which it enters." Reading {to de kalon ekhoimen an pos allos eipein e estin onomazein kalon e soma e skeuos e all' otioun, o oistha pros tanta kalon on; Ma Di', ouk egog', ephe}. For other emendations of the vulg., and the many interpretations which have been given to the passage, see R. Kuhner ad loc.

Euth. I confess I do not know of any such myself.[27]

[27] Or, adopting the reading {ekhois an} in place of {ekhoimen an} above, translate "I certainly cannot, I confess."

Soc. I presume to turn a thing to its proper use is to apply it beautifully?
Euth. Undoubtedly it is a beautiful appliance.[28]

[28] Or, "I presume it is well and good and beautiful to use this, that, and the other thing for the purpose for which the particular thing is useful?" - "That nobody can deny (he answered)." It is impossible to convey simply the verbal play and the quasi- argumentative force of the Greek {kalos ekhei pros ti tini khresthai}. See K. Joel, p. 426.

Soc. And is this, that, and the other thing beautiful for aught else except that to which it may be beautifully applied?
Euth. No single thing else.
Soc. It would seem that the useful is beautiful relatively to that for which it is of use?
So it appears to me (he answered).

Soc. And what of courage,[29] Euthydemus? I presume you rank courage among things beautiful? It is a noble quality?[30]

[29] Or, perhaps better, "fortitude." See H. Sidgwick, "Hist. of Ethics," p. 43.
[30] It is one of {ta kala}. See K. Joel, ib. p. 325, and in reference to the definitions of the Good and of the Beautiful, ib. p. 425 foll.

Nay, one of the most noble (he answered).
Soc. It seems that you regard courage as useful to no mean end?
Euth. Nay, rather the greatest of all ends, God knows.
Soc. Possibly in face of terrors and dangers you would consider it an advantage to be ignorant of them?
Certainly not (he answered).
Soc. It seems that those who have no fear in face of dangers, simply because they do not know what they are, are not courageous?
Most true (he answered); or, by the same showing, a large proportion of madmen and cowards would be courageous.
Soc. Well, and what of those who are in dread of things which are not dreadful, are they -
Euth. Courageous, Socrates? - still less so than the former, goodness knows.
Soc. Possibly, then, you would deem those who are good in the face of terrors and dangers to be courageous, and those who are bad in the face of the same to be cowards?
Certainly I should (he answered).
Soc. And can you suppose any other people to be good in respect of such things except those who are able to cope with them and turn them to noble account?[31]

[31] {kalos khresthai}, lit. "make a beautiful use of them."

No; these and these alone (he answered).
Soc. And those people who are of a kind to cope but badly with the same occurrences, it would seem, are bad?
Who else, if not they? (he asked).
Soc. May it be that both one and the other class do use these circumstances as they think they must and should?[32]

[32] Or, "feel bound and constrained to do."

Why, how else should they deal with them? (he asked).
Soc. Can it be said that those who are unable to cope well with them or to turn them to noble account know how they must and should deal with them?[33]

[33] Or, "Can it be said that those who are unable to cope nobly with their perilous surroundings know how they ought to deal with them?"

I presume not (he answered).
Soc. It would seem to follow that those who have the knowledge how to behave are also those who have the power?[34]

[34] "He who kens can."

Yes; these, and these alone (he said).

Soc. Well, but now, what of those who have made no egregious blunder (in the matter); can it be they cope ill with the things and circumstances we are discussing?

I think not (he answered).

Soc. It would seem, conversely, that they who cope ill have made some egregious blunder?

Euth. Probably; indeed, it would appear to follow.

Soc. It would seem, then, that those who know[35] how to cope with terrors and dangers well and nobly are courageous, and those who fail utterly of this are cowards?

[35] "Who have the {episteme}."

So I judge them to be (he answered).[36]

[36] N.B. - For this definition of courage see Plat. "Laches," 195 A and passim; K. Joel, op. cit. p. 325 foll.

A kingdom and a tyrranny[37] were, he opined, both of them forms of government, but forms which differed from one another, in his belief; a kingdom was a government over willing men in accordance with civil law, whereas a tyranny implied the government over unwilling subjects not according to law, but so as to suit the whims and wishes of the ruler.

[37] Or, "despotism."

There were, moreover, three forms of citizenship or polity; in the case where the magistrates were appointed from those who discharged the obligations prescribed by law, he held the polity to be an aristocracy (or rule of the best);[38] where the title to office depended on rateable property, it was a plutocracy (or rule of wealth); and lastly, where all the citizens without distinction held the reins of office, that was a democracy (or rule of the people).

[38] Or, "in which the due discharge of lawful (law-appointed) obligations gave the title to magisterial office and government, this form of polity he held to be an aristocracy (or rule of the best)." See Newman, op. cit. i. 212, 235.

Let me explain his method of reply where the disputant had no clear statement to make, but without attempt at proof chose to contend that such or such a person named by himself was wiser, or more of a statesman, or more courageous, and so forth, than some other person.[39] Socrates had a way of bringing the whole discussion back to the underlying proposition,[40] as thus:

[39] Or, "if any one encountered him in argument about any topic or person without any clear statement, but a mere ipse dixit, devoid of demonstration, that so and so," etc.
[40] Or, "question at bottom." Cf. Plat. "Laws," 949 B.

Soc. You state that so and so, whom you admire, is a better citizen that this other whom I admire?

The Disputant. Yes; I repeat the assertion.

Soc. But would it not have been better to inquire first what is the work or function of a good citizen?

The Disputant. Let us do so.

Soc. To begin, then, with the matter of expenditure: his superiority will be shown by his increasing the resources and lightening the expenditure of the state?[41]

[41] Or, "In the management of moneys, then, his strength will consist in his rendering the state better provided with ways and means?"

Certainly (the disputant would answer).

Soc. And in the event of war, by rendering his state superior to her antagonists?

The Disputant. Clearly.

Soc. Or on an embassy as a diplomatist, I presume, by securing friends in place of enemies?

That I should imagine (replies the disputant).

Soc. Well, and in parliamentary debate, by putting a stop to party strife and fostering civic concord?

The Disputant. That is my opinion.

By this method of bringing back the argument to its true starting- point, even the disputant himself would be affected and the truth become manifest to his mind.

His own - that is, the Socratic - method of conducting a rational discussion[42] was to proceed step by step from one point of general agreement to another: "Herein lay the real security of reasoning,"[43] he would say; and for this reason he was more successful in winning the common assent of his hearers than any one I ever knew. He had a saying that Homer had conferred on Odyesseus the title of a safe, unerring orator,[44] because he had the gift to lead the discussion from one commonly accepted opinion to another.

[42] Of, "of threading the mazes of an argument."

[43] Reading {tauton asphaleian}; aliter. {tauten ten asphaleian} = "that this security was part and parcel of reasoning."

[44] "Od." viii. 171, {o d' asphaleos agoreuei}, "and his speech runs surely on its way" (Butcher and Lang), where Odysseus is describing himself. Cf. Dion. Hal. "de Arte Rhet." xi. 8.

VII

The frankness and simplicity with which Socrates endeavoured to declare his own opinions, in dealing with those who conversed with him,[1] is, I think, conclusively proved by the above instances; at the same time, as I hope now to show, he was no less eager to cultivate a spirit of independence in others, which would enable them to stand alone in all transactions suited to their powers.

[1] Or, "who frequented his society, is, I hope, clear from what has been said."

Of all the men I have ever known, he was most anxious to ascertain in what any of those about him was really versed; and within the range of his own knowledge he showed the greatest zeal in teaching everything which it befits the true gentleman[2] to know; or where he was deficient in knowledge himself,[3] he would introduce his friends to those who knew.[4] He did not fail to teach them also up to what point it was proper for an educated man to acquire empiric knowledge of any particular matter.[5]

[2] Lit. "a beautiful and good man."
[3] Or, "where he lacked acquaintance with the matter himself." See, for an instance, "Econ." iii. 14.
[4] "To those who had the special knowledge"; "a connoisseur in the matter."
[5] Or, "of any particular branch of learning"; "in each department of things."

To take geometry as an instance: Every one (he would say) ought to be taught geometry so far, at any rate, as to be able, if necessary, to take over or part with a piece of land, or to divide it up or assign a portion of it for cultivation,[6] and in every case by geometric rule.[7] That amount of geometry was so simple indeed, and easy to learn, that it only needed ordinary application of the mind to the method of mensuration, and the student could at once ascertain the size of the piece of land, and, with the satisfaction of knowing its measurement, depart in peace. But he was unable to approve of the pursuit of geometry up to the point at which it became a study of unintelligible diagrams.[8] What the use of these might be, he failed, he said, to see; and yet he was not unversed in these recondite matters himself.[9] These things, he would say, were enough to wear out a man's life, and to hinder him from many other more useful studies.[10]

[6] {e ergon apodeixasthai}, or "and to explain the process." Cf. Plat. "Rep." vii. 528 D. See R. Kuhner ad loc. for other interpretations of the phrase. Cf. Max. Tyr. xxxvii. 7.

[7] Or, "by correct measurement"; lit. "by measurement of the earth."

[8] Cf. Aristot. "Pol." v. (viii.) 2; Cic. "Acad. Post." I. iv. 15. For the attitude compare the attitude of a philosopher in other respects most unlike Socrates - August Comte, e.g. as to the futility of sidereal astronomy, "Pos. Pol." i. 412 (Bridges).

[9] Cf. Isocr. "On the Antidosis," 258-269, as to the true place of "Eristic" in education. See above, IV. ii. 10.

[10] Cf. A. Comte as to "perte intellectuelle" in the pursuit of barren studies.

Again, a certain practical knowledge of astronomy, a certain skill in the study of the stars, he strongly insisted on. Every one should know enough of the science to be able to discover the hour of the night or the season of the month or year, for the purposes of travel by land or sea - the march, the voyage, and the regulations of the watch;[11] and in general, with regard to all matters connected with the night season, or with the month, or the year,[12] it was well to have such reliable data to go upon as would serve to distinguish the various times and seasons. But these, again, were pieces of knowledge easily learnt from night sportsmen,[13] pilots of vessels, and many others who make it their business to know such things. As to pushing the study of astronomy so far as to include a knowledge of the movements of bodies outside our own orbit, whether planets or stars of eccentric movement,[14] or wearing oneself out endeavouring to discover their distances from the earth, their periods, and their causes,[15] all this he strongly discountenanced; for he saw (he said) no advantage in these any more than in the former studies. And yet he was not unversed[16] in the subtleties of astronomy any more than in those of geometry; only these, again, he insisted, were sufficient to wear out a man's lifetime, and to keep him away from many more useful pursuits.

[11] Schneid. cf. Plat. "Rep." vii. 527 D.

[12] "Occurrences connected with the night, the month, or year." e.g. the festival of the Karneia, the {tekmerion} (point de repere) of which is the full moon of August. Cf. Eur. "Alc." 449.

[13] See Plat. "Soph." 220 D; above, III. xi. 8; "Cyrop." I. vi. 40; "Hunting," xii. 6; Hippocr. "Aer." 28.

[14] See Lewis, "Astron. of the Ancients"; cf. Diog. Laert. vii. 1. 144.

[15] Or, "the causes of these."

[16] {oude touton ge anekoos en}. He had "heard," it is said, Archelaus, a pupil of Anaxagoras. Cf. Cic. "Tusc." V. iv. 10.

And to speak generally, in regard of things celestial he set his face against attempts to excogitate the machinery by which the divine power formed its several operations.[17] Not only were these matters beyond man's faculties to discover, as he believed, but the attempt to search out what the gods had not chosen to reveal could hardly (he supposed) be well pleasing in their sight. Indeed, the man who tortured his brains about such subjects stood a fair chance of losing his wits entirely, just as Anaxagoras,[18] the headiest speculator of them all, in his attempt to explain the divine mechanism, had somewhat lost his head. Anaxagoras took on himself to assert that sun and fire are identical,[19] ignoring the fact that human beings can easily look at fire, but to gaze steadily into the face of the sun is given to no man; or that under the influence of his rays the colour of the skin changes, but under the rays of fire not.[20] He forgot that no plant or vegetation springs from earth's bosom with healthy growth without the help of sunlight, whilst the influence of fire is to parch up everything, and to destroy life; and when he came to speak of the sun as being a "red-hot stone" he ignored another fact, that a stone in fire neither lights up nor lasts, whereas the sun-god abides for ever with intensest brilliancy undimmed.

[17] Or, "he tried to divert one from becoming overly-wise in heavenly matters and the 'mecanique celeste' of the Godhead in His several operations." See above, I. i. 11. See Grote, "Plato," i. 438.

[18] Of Clazomenae. Cf. Plat. "Apol." 14; Diog. Laert. II. vi; Cic. "Tusc." V. iv. 10; Cobet, "Prosop. Xen." s.n.; Grote, "H. G." i. 501.

[19] Or, "that the sun was simply a fire, forgetting so simple a fact as that."

[20] Or, "the complexion darkens, whereas fire has no such effect."

Socrates inculcated the study of reasoning processes,[21] but in these, equally with the rest, he bade the student beware of vain and idle over-occupation. Up to the limit set by utility, he was ready to join in any investigation, and to follow out an argument with those who were with him; but there he stopped. He particularly urged those who were with him to pay the utmost attention to health. They would learn all it was possible to learn from adepts, and not only so, but each one individually should take pains to discover, by a lifelong observation of his own case, what particular regimen, what meat or drink, or what kind of work, best suited him; these he should turn to account with a view to leading the healthiest possible life. It would be no easy matter for any one who would follow this advice, and study his own idiosyncrasy, to find a doctor to improve either on the diagnosis or the treatment requisite.[22]

[21] {logismous} = (1) "arithmetic," (2) "calculation," (3) "syllogistic reasoning." See L. Dind. "Index. Gr." s.v., and Kuhner ad loc.; cf. Plat. "Gorg." 451 C. It is important to decide which form of "logism" is meant here.

[22] Or, "to find a doctor better able than himself to 'diagnose' and prescribe a treatment congenial to health." Cf. Tac. "Ann." vi. 46; Plut. "de San." 136 E, ap. Schneid. ad loc.

Where any one came seeking for help which no human wisdom could supply, he would counsel him to give heed to "divination." He who has the secret of the means whereby the gods give signs to men touching their affairs can never surely find himself bereft of heavenly guidance.

VIII

Now if any one should be disposed to set the statement of Socrates touching the divinity[1] which warned him what he ought to do or not to do, against the fact that he was sentenced to death by the board of judges, and argue that thereby Socrates stood convicted of lying and delusion in respect of this "divinity" of his, I would have him to note in the first place that, at the date of his trial, Socrates was already so far advanced in years that had he not died then his life would have reached its natural term soon afterwards; and secondly, as matters went, he escaped life's bitterest load[2] in escaping those years which bring a diminution of intellectual force to all - instead of which he was called upon to exhibit the full robustness of his soul and acquire glory in addition,[3] partly by the style of his defence - felicitous alike in its truthfulness, its freedom, and its rectitude[4] - and partly by the manner in which he bore the sentence of condemnation with infinite gentleness and manliness. Since no one within the memory of man, it is admitted, ever bowed his head to death more nobly. After the sentence he must needs live for thirty days, since it was the month of the "Delia,"[5] and the law does not suffer any man to die by the hand of the public executioner until the sacred embassy return from Delos. During the whole of that period (as his acquaintances without exception can testify) his life proceeded as usual. There was nothing to mark the difference between now and formerly in the even tenour of its courage; and it was a life which at all times had been a marvel of cheerfulness and calm content.[6]

[1] Or, "the words of Socrates with regard to a divine something which warned him," etc.
[2] The phraseology is poetical.
[3] Or, "in a manner which redounded to his glory."
[4] Or, "marvellous alike for the sincerity of its language, the free unbroken spirit of its delivery, and the absolute rectitude of the speaker."
[5] i.e. the lesser "Delian" solemnities, an annual festival instituted, it was said, by Theseus. See Plut. "Theseus," 23 (Clough, i. 19); and for the whole matter see Plat. "Phaed." 58 foll.
[6] Cf. Arist. "Frogs," 82; of Sophocles, {o d' eukolos men enthad', eukolos d' ekei}.

[Let us pause and ask how could man die more nobly and more beautifully than in the way described? or put it thus: dying so, then was his death most noble and most beautiful; and being the most beautiful, then was it also the most fortunate and heaven-blest; and being most blessed of heaven, then was it also most precious in the sight of God.][7]

[7] This is bracketed as spurious by Sauppe and other commentators. But see "Cyrop." VIII. ii. 7, 8, for similar ineptitude of style. R. Kuhner defends the passage as genuine.

And now I will mention further certain things which I have heard from Hermogenes, the son of Hipponicus,[8] concerning him. He said that even after Meletus[9] had drawn up the indictment, he himself used to hear Socrates conversing and discussing everything rather than the suit impending, and had ventured to suggest that he ought to be considering the line of his defence, to which, in the first instance, the master answered: "Do I not seem to you to have been practising that my whole life long?" And upon his asking "How?" added in explanation that he had passed his days in nothing else save in distinguishing between what is just and what is unjust (right and wrong), and in doing what is right and abstaining from what is wrong; "which conduct" (he added) "I hold to be the finest possible practice for my defence"; and when he (Hermogenes), returning to the point again, pleaded with Socrates: "Do you not see, Socrates, how commonly it happens that an Athenian jury, under the influence of argument, condemns innocent people to death and acquits real criminals?" - Socrates replied, "I assure you, Hermogenes, that each time I have essayed to give my thoughts to the defence which I am to make before the court, the divinity[10] has opposed me." And when he (Hermogenes) exclaimed, "How strange!" - "Do you find it strange" (he continued), "that to the Godhead it should appear better for me to close my life at once? Do you not know that up to the present moment there is no man whom I can admit to have spent a better or happier life than mine. Since theirs I regard as the best of lives who study best to become as good as may be, and theirs the happiest who have the liveliest sense of growth in goodness; and such, hitherto, is the happy fortune which I perceive to have fallen to my lot. To such conclusion I have come, not only in accidental intercourse with others, but by a strict comparison drawn between myself and others, and in this faith I continue to this day; and not I only, but my friends continue in a like persuasion with regard to me, not for the lame reason that they are my friends and love me (or else would others have been in like case as regards their friends), but because they are persuaded that by being with me they will attain to their full height of goodness. But, if I am destined to prolong my days, maybe I shall be enforced to pay in full the penalties of old age - to see and hear less keenly, to fail in intellectual force, and to leave school, as it were, more of a dunce than when I came, less learned and more forgetful - in a word, I shall fall from my high estate, and daily grow worse in that wherein aforetime I excelled. But indeed, were it possible to remain unconscious of the change, the life left would scarcely be worth living; but given that there is a consciousness of the change, then must the existence left to live be found by comparison insipid, joyless, a death in life, devoid of life's charm. But indeed, if it is reserved for me to die unjustly, then on those who unjustly slay me lies the shame [since, given injustice is base, how can any unjust action whatsoever fail of baseness?][11] But for me what disgrace is it that others should fail of a just decision and right acts concerning me? . . . I see before me a long line of predecessors on this road, and I mark the reputation also among posterity which they have left.[12] I note how it varies according as they did or suffered wrong, and for myself I know that I too, although I die to-day, shall obtain from mankind a consideration far different from that which will be accorded to those who put me to death. I know that undying witness will be borne me to this effect, that I never at any time did wrong to any man, or made him a worse man, but ever tried to make those better who were with me."

[8] See above, II. x. 3; "Symp." i. 3; iii. 14; iv. 47 foll.; vi. 2; "Apol." 2; Plat. "Crat." 384.
[9] See above, I. i. 1.
[10] {to daimonion} - "the divine (voice)."
[11] This passage also may, perhaps, be regarded as spurious.
[12] Or, "There floats before my eyes a vision of the many who have gone this same gate. I note their legacies of fame among posterity."

Such are the words which he spoke in conversation with Hermogenes and the rest. But amongst those who knew Socrates and recognised what manner of man he was, all who make virtue and perfection their pursuit still to this day cease not to lament his loss with bitterest regret, as for one who helped them in the pursuit of virtue as none else could.

To me, personally, he was what I have myself endeavoured to describe: so pious and devoutly religious[13] that he would take no step apart from the will of heaven; so just and upright that he never did even a trifling injury to any living soul; so self-controlled, so temperate, that he never at any time chose the sweeter in place of the better; so sensible, and wise, and prudent that in distinguishing the better from the worse he never erred; nor had he need of any helper, but for the knowledge of these matters, his judgment was at once infallible and self-sufficing. Capable of reasonably setting forth and defining moral questions,[14] he was also able to test others, and where they erred, to cross-examine and convict them, and so to impel and guide them in the path of virtue and noble manhood. With these characteristics, he seemed to be the very impersonation of human perfection and happiness.[15]

[13] Or, "of such piety and religious devotedness . . . of such rectitude . . . of such sobreity and self-control . . . of such sound sense and wisdom . . ."
[14] Or, "gifted with an ability logically to set forth and to define moral subtleties."
[15] Or, "I look upon him as at once the best and happiest of men."
Such is our estimate. If the verdict fail to satisfy I would ask those who disagree with it to place the character of any other side by side with this delineation, and then pass sentence.

Printed in Great Britain
by Amazon